John Falconar Slater

The North East's Weatherproof Artist

Tyne
Bridge
Publishing

Dedicated to the memory of
Agnes Dorothy Slater
(1900-1992)
without whose kind assistance
this brief biography
of her father
could not have been written

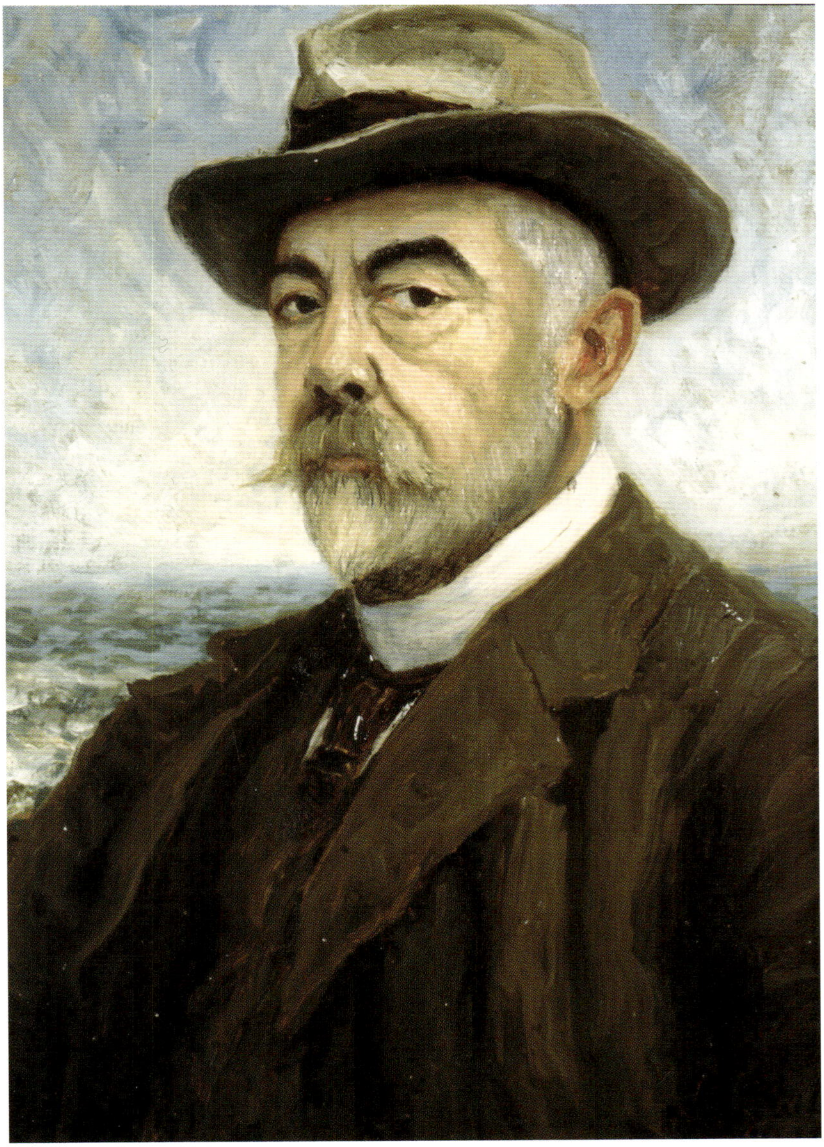

John Falconar Slater 1857 – 1937. A self portrait, aged 70
(Anderson & Garland)

John Falconar Slater

The North East's Weatherproof Artist

Marshall Hall

ISBN: 978-1-838280918

Published by:
City of Newcastle Upon Tyne
Newcastle Libraries
Tyne Bridge Publishing, 2021
unless otherwise indicated
Layout design: Derek Tree

Also by Marshall Hall:
The Artists of Northumbria, 1973, 1982, and 2005;
The Artists of Cumbria, 1979;
Newcastle between the Wars, 2011.

Contents

Acknowledgements

Second only to the help received from John Falconar Slater's daughter Agnes Dorothy in preparing this biography of her father, has been the assistance of the artist's great niece Coralie Gilmour, whose recent contact with me from her home in Queensland, Australia, has enabled me to confirm, or enlarge upon, many details regarding his family.

Others whose help I should like to acknowledge are the late George Lilly, director of the Vicarage Cottage Gallery, North Shields, for permitting me to use his introduction to the Gallery's 1987 exhibition of Slater's work as an introduction to this volume; Peter Walton, artist and distant member of the Slater family, and Geoff Nicholson, for their help in my initial genealogical researches; North Tyneside Public Libraries Local Studies for providing me with access to its records of the artist's life and work; Newcastle upon Tyne auctioneers Anderson & Garland for enabling me to familiarise myself with literally dozens of examples of Slater's work passing through its saleroom over an almost twenty-year period, and for permission to reproduce selected examples; the Laing Art Gallery, Newcastle upon Tyne, for allowing me to reproduce some important examples of the artist's work in its permanent collection; Ian Sharp Antiques, formerly of Tynemouth, for help in pursuing several lines of enquiry about Slater works handled by the business over the years, and last, but not least, Newcastle City Libraries Local Studies for its help in answering many of my queries, and permitting me to use several images from its large collection of photographs of the city.

Foreword

My interest in John Falconar Slater began in 1971 when I commenced the preparation of an entry on the artist for the first edition of my dictionary of North East artists – *The Artists of Northumbria*, published in 1973. Little was known of Slater's life and career as an artist at that time save what had been briefly stated in various catalogues of the Laing Art Gallery, Newcastle.

This situation still prevailed when the second edition of my book was published in 1982. By a happy coincidence, however, shortly after this edition was published I learnt that the artist's daughter Agnes Dorothy (she always preferred just 'Dorothy') had moved to live only a quarter of a mile from my then home at Ryton, in the Tyne Valley. I introduced myself, and then met regularly with her over the few years she remained there, inevitably talking about her father and his career as an artist. Photographs, letters and other memorabilia relating to these matters were discussed, and in some instances copied, or donated to my files.

Gradually the idea of one day producing a biography of her father developed. However, much would have to be researched and documented to supplement Dorothy's recollections of her father, valuable as these would later prove to be, and the distraction meanwhile of tackling other writing commitments, including several other artist biographies for the *New Oxford Dictionary of National Biography*, published in 2004, the updating and enlargement of my third edition of *The Artists of Northumbria*, published in 2005, and a study of the newspaper illustrations of my one-time art tutor Byron Dawson, published in 2011, as *Newcastle between the Wars*, proved welcome but time-consuming distractions.

This time was not, however, wasted in terms of further researching Slater's work as an artist. During most of this period I was retained by leading North East Fine Art Auctioneers Anderson & Garland, to assist in the valuation (and in several instances the authentication) of literally dozens of Slater's oils, watercolours and gouaches, discovering much about his work in the process.

The impetus to finally complete the book came with the news in 2012 that a commemorative plaque was to be placed on the artist's one-time home at Cullercoats. The spontaneous media interest which this event generated, and the consequent public demand to know more about the man honoured in this way, left little doubt that this task would be one well worth completing, however much further research into his life and work might be required.

In the event its completion happily coincides with the centenary of Slater's most important contribution to the artistic life of the region outside his painting – his creation of The North East Coast Art Club in 1920. Surviving for more than 40 years it enabled dozens of aspiring local artists to receive tuition at its classes and go on to successfully exhibit their work.

Marshall Hall 2020

Introduction

John Falconar Slater was born in 1857 and died 80 years later in 1937. His life thus spanned the hey-day of the British Empire. The year of his birth followed hard on the Crimean War and the Indian Mutiny, and the year of his death was similarly close to the outbreak of the Second World War.

In the world of art the Pre-Raphaelites were controversially ascendant in England when he was born, and when he began to paint seriously in the 1880s the Glasgow Boys, representing another challenge to the mainstream of Victorian Art, were getting into their stride; in France, Monet was at the height of his powers.

In the year of Slater's death Picasso painted his famous Guernica, a major historical and artistic document of the 20th century, and by that time numerous modernist schools had arrived – and a good few of them had already gone. Of course Slater's name is not mentioned in the same breath as these illustrious artists in order to place him on the same exalted plane but to recall the many and varied influences at work in the development of painting during his long life, and to remind us that he was a great absorber and great experimenter.

Those, now very few in number, who remember Slater mostly have an image of an elderly, rather Edwardian figure, working against the odds and despite the elements " en plein air", and tirelessly recording the shorelines of Cullercoats, Tynemouth and Whitley Bay, ever fascinated by the constantly changing play of light on water and rock.

These coastal subjects were certainly a major interest of Slater but he had numerous others. Misty moorlands abound in his work, as do colourful cottage gardens, bright compositions of farmyard animals and haystacks, and quiet pastoral scenes in a naturalist manner. The technique and style vary enormously as well as the subject. The fine glaze-work and meticulous delineation normal in fine classical 19th century painting and evident still in the work of that other Northumbrian artist Ralph Hedley, are hardly seen in Slater's pictures. He was adventurous and experimental in using at times the heaviest impasto, at times impressionist and divisionist techniques, more rarely a thin scumble giving an almost wash-like effect. In all an individual amalgam of the traditional and avant-garde.

Now, these many years since his death, we can see Slater as probably the most innovative of local painters of the period, an immensely enthusiastic and prolific artist painting indefatigably, trying many things – new subjects, new styles – not always succeeding, but in his overall achievement showing himself as is now more widely being recognised beyond his native heath, as a genuine talent, the first modern Northumbrian artist.

George Lilly, Director, Vicarage Cottage Gallery, North Shields

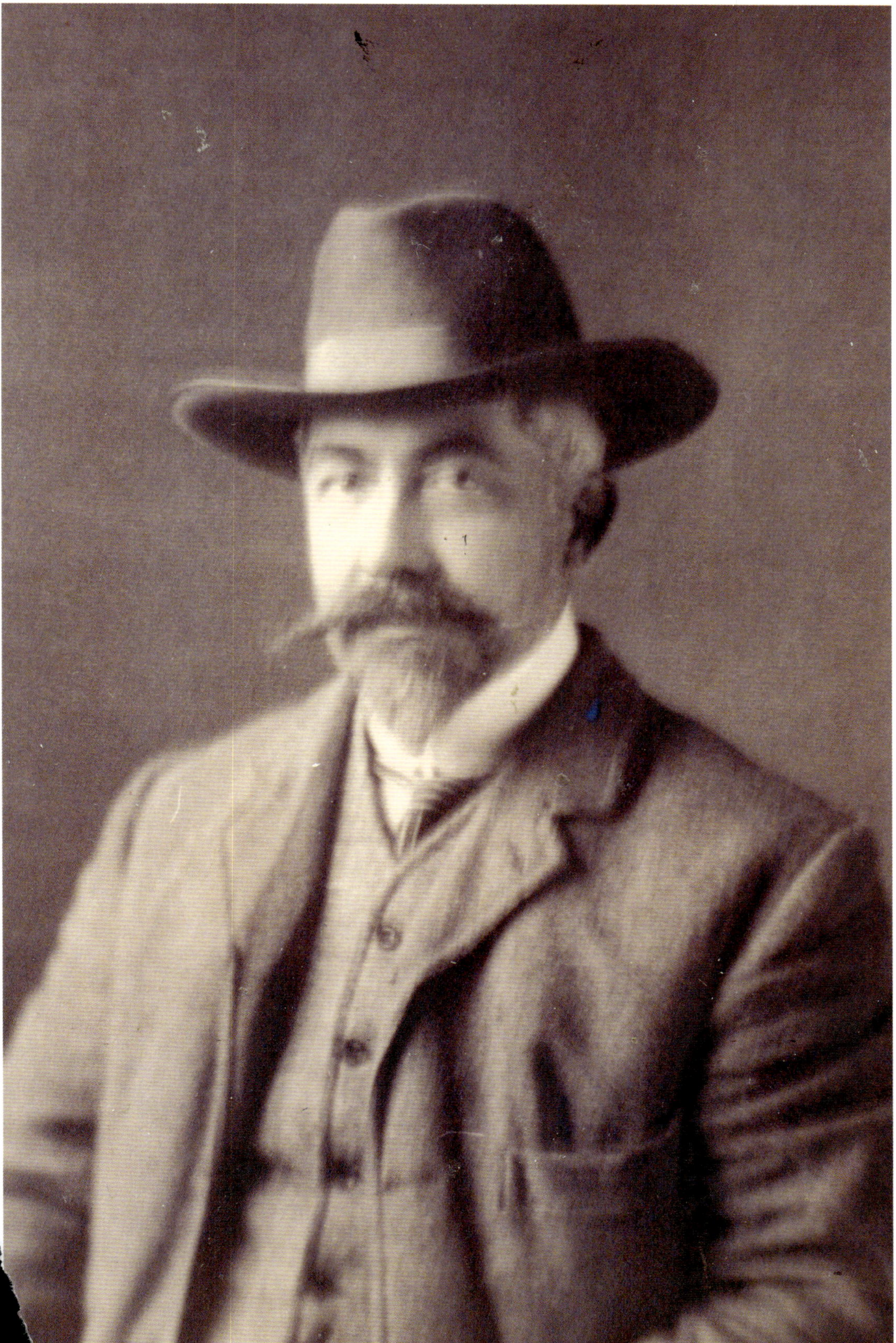

A Miller's Son

Chapter One

John Falconar Slater was born on the 26th March, 1857[1] into a family of millers that had been in business on Tyneside for generations. His father Thomas had run its Newcastle mill since joining it as a young man and, by the time Slater was born, had become sole proprietor, living comfortably with his wife Mary, daughter Mary, and first son Thomas, in Elswick West Terrace, a short distance from the mill, at what is today called Rye Hill.

Slater's earliest recollections of the mill were of an old stone and timber building standing in the shadow of the town's recently constructed Central Station. And it was to him a place of noise and excitement, where the clanking of its steam-operated milling machinery mingled with the cries of wagoners as they manoeuvred their cargoes of grain from Forth Street into the yard abutting the mill.

Later, when he had started at a small private school near his home, he began to make pencil sketches of this scene, his eyes drawn to the teams of powerful horses with their brass-mounted harnesses. Later still, he would be allowed to add his own subjects to the scene – a collection of gaily-coloured English gamecocks. Draught horses and gamecocks would remain two of his favourite subjects throughout his subsequent career as an artist, although only one person during his boyhood realised the promise of his early drawings.

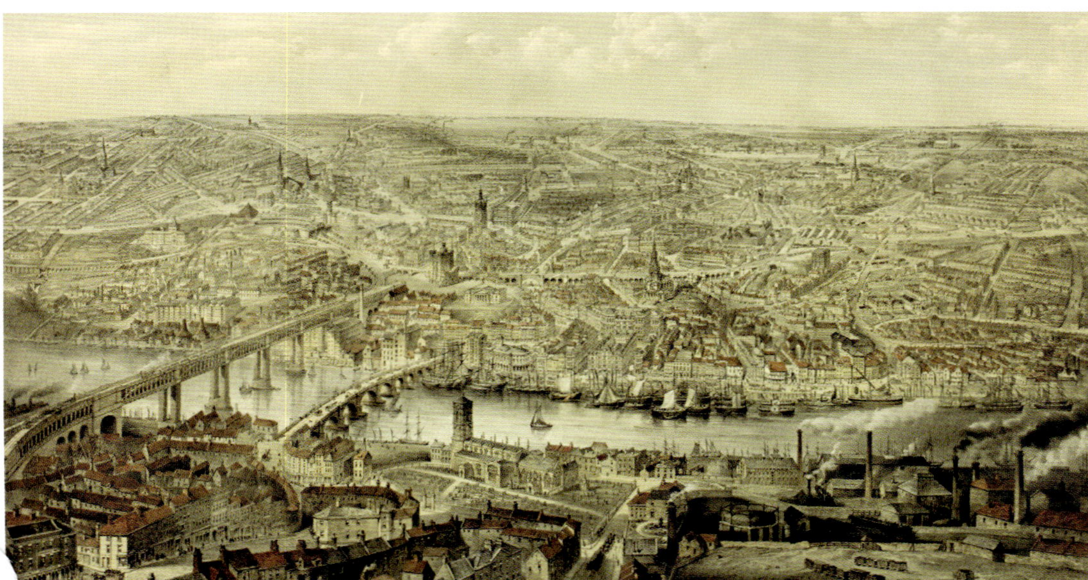

? Newcastle of Slater's childhood, from a lithograph by John Storey (1828-1888), dated 1862.

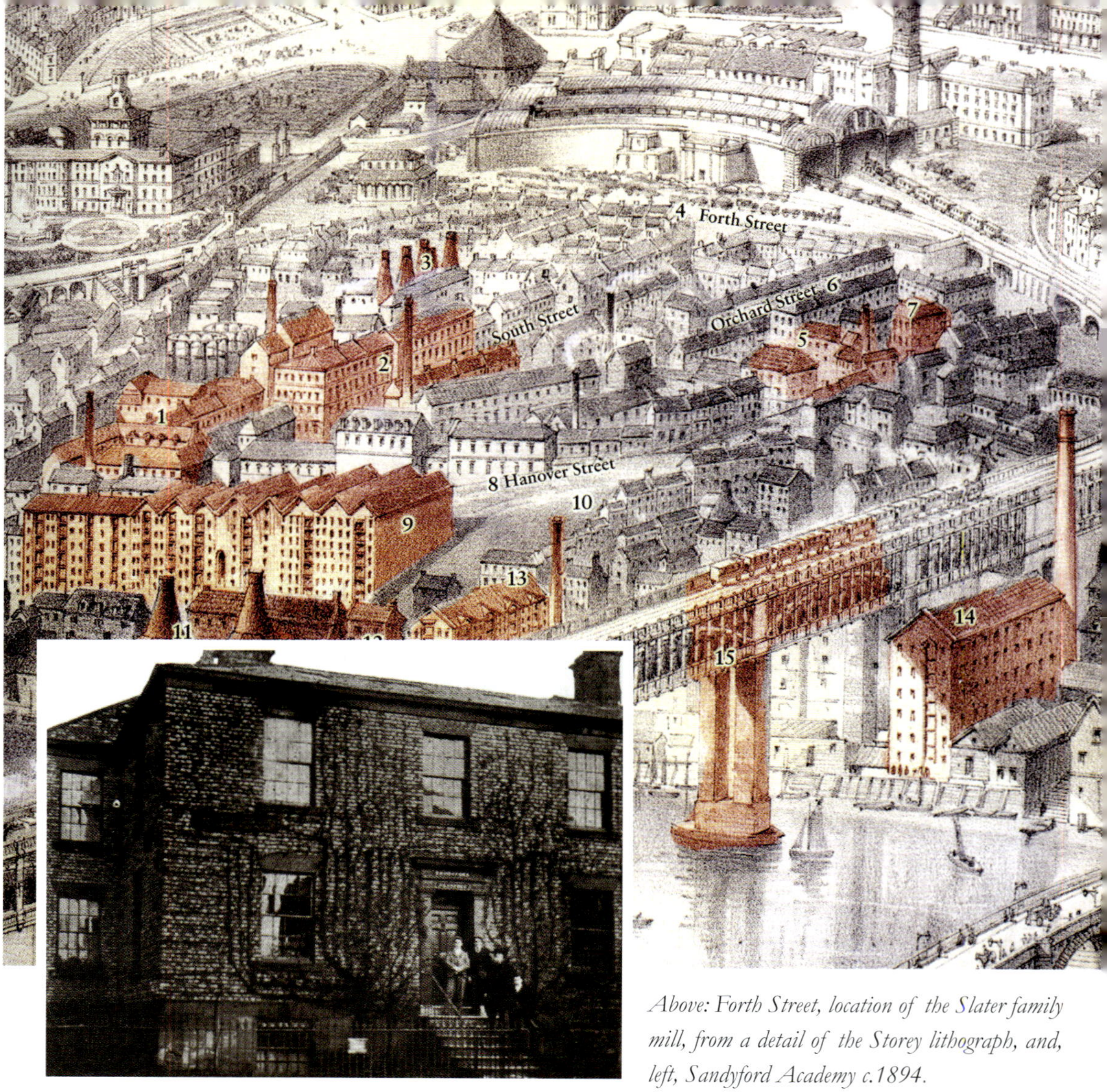

Above: Forth Street, location of the Slater family mill, from a detail of the Storey lithograph, and, left, Sandyford Academy c.1894.

Said this well-known local critic: "This child's work will one day hang in the Royal Academy, London." And by a strange turn of events this critic's son, without knowing of his father's prediction, bought one of Slater's Royal Academy pictures many years afterwards. But Slater thought little of his skill at drawing in these early years, and despite encouragement from his artistically talented mother could only think of one day becoming a farmer.

His father had other ideas, however, and when he was twelve enrolled him as a pupil in the newly opened Sandyford Academy on the corner of Nixon Street and Sandyford Road in the Jesmond area of the town. The family, now joined by brother Waldron Story (b.1859), and sisters Margaret Falconar (b.1861), Bertha (b.1864), and Edith Maud (b.1868)[2], had by then moved from increasingly populous Elswick, to more genteel Hunter's Terrace in Jesmond, and Slater's education at the Academy was clearly designed to fit him as the son of a gentleman working in the family business.

The Academy taught him well. It had been established in 1869 by one Robert Wilson, described in *The Illustrated Chronicle* a quarter of a century later as "a sound educationalist of the new school, and a member of Edinburgh University Council, whose deep acquaintance with ancient and modern literature, added to extensive Continental experiences, give him great advantages as a preceptor of youth." Slater became one of its first pupils, and by the time he left it aged sixteen it had already established a reputation for giving students "a thoroughly practical education"[3].

Indeed, the degree to which his education at the Academy shaped his later attitudes must have been considerable. Continued the piece in *The Illustrated Chronicle*: "It will be seen that he (Wilson) has altogether eschewed the public school system of making each pupil in a certain groove, and spend valuable time in the pursuit of studies that will be useless to him in after life." Slater certainly could not ever have been thought to be in a 'certain groove', as both artist and man. But, although this education might easily have equipped him to go on to university, he was persuaded to join his father's mill as a clerk with a view to eventually running it.

While studying at the Academy, and perhaps encouraged by its Principal, Slater began to take an interest in Newcastle's history, discovering among many things that Thomas Bewick had once been a resident of the area around his father's mill – in fact just on the other side of the Central Station, where a street named after the engraver had since been built. And, of course, as he quickly discovered on reading up on the town's development since Bewick earlier in the

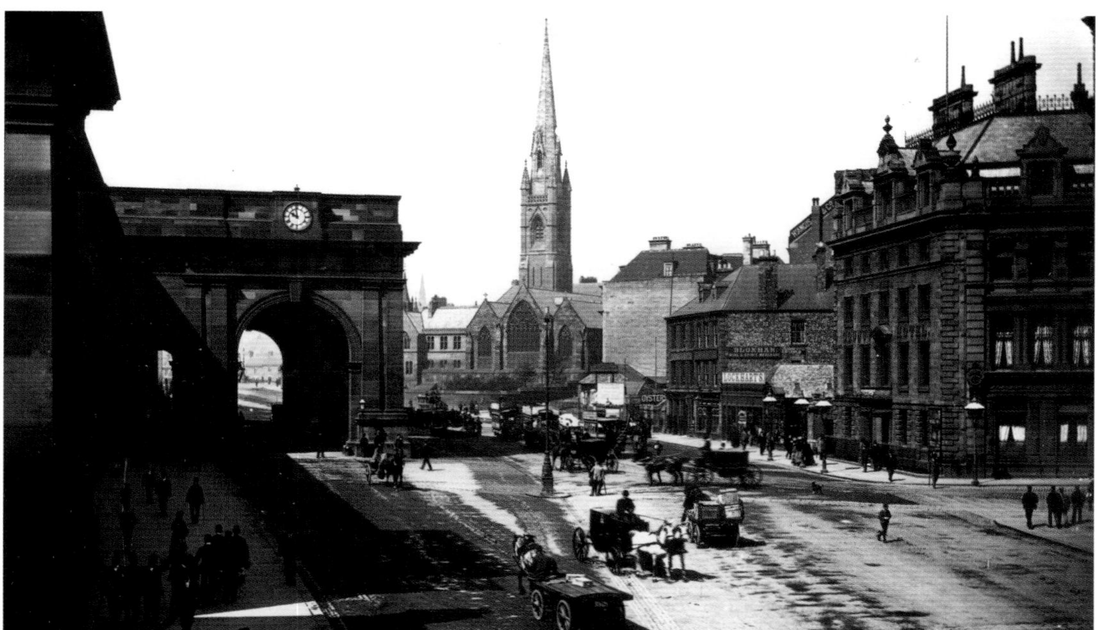

Newcastle's Central Station as it looked at the turn of the century. The horse-drawn carriage in the foreground was probably owned by one of Slater's relatives who operated a cab service from the station.

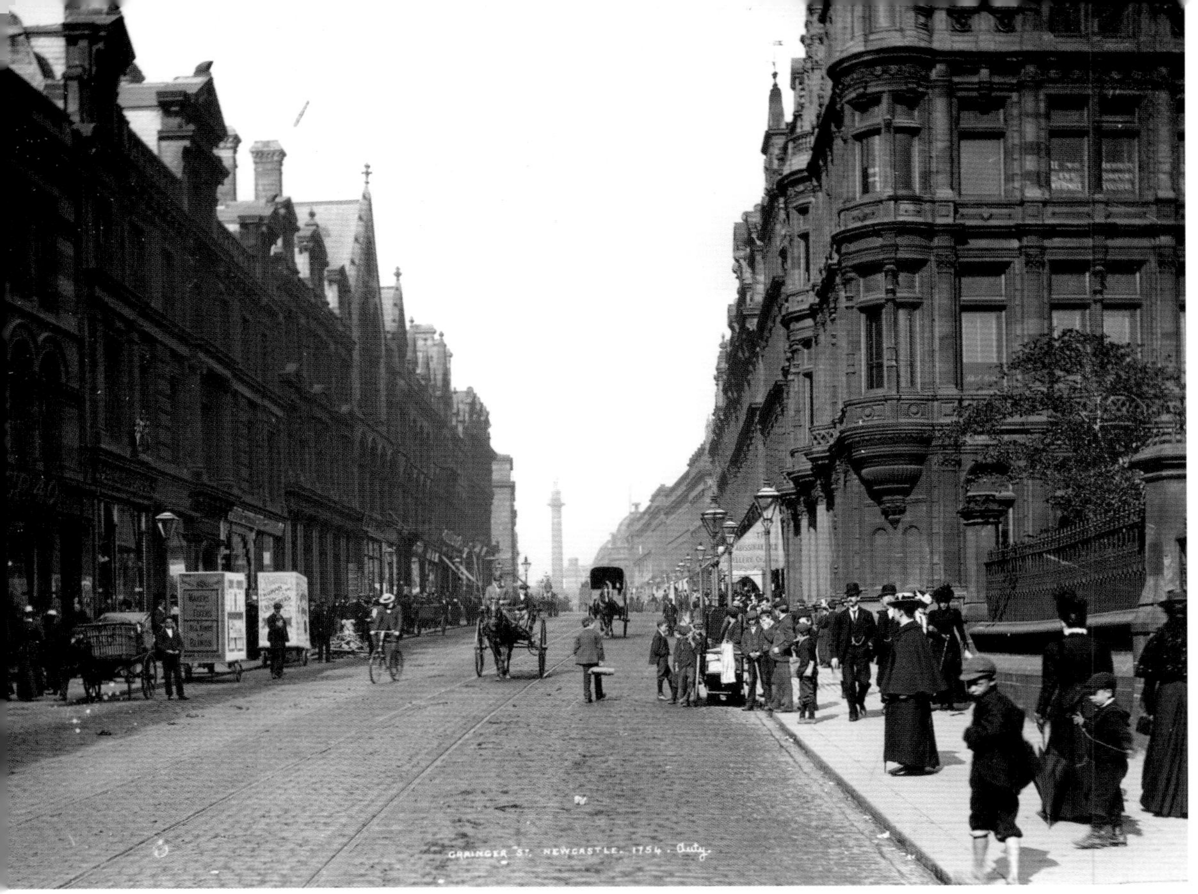

Grainger Street, Newcastle, part of the city's major redevelopment in the early 19th century.

century had left his 'little cot at the Forth', to live at Gateshead, much else had changed in Newcastle's streetscape, largely due to the enterprise of one Richard Grainger.

He discovered several of the streets he now walked down on his way to the mill since they had moved from Rye Hill had only a few decades previously been rebuilt by Grainger: Grey Street, Grainger Street, and Clayton Street, to name only three. And, quite independent of his enterprise, much of Newcastle's Quayside had been rebuilt following the catastrophic fire that had broken out in Gateshead three years before Slater had been born, and spread to that location. All in all he began to take a pride in this town, not yet the city it would become in 1882 when he was newly returned from his 'wanderlust' period in South Africa.

Within a few years of his having joined the mill at 8 Forth Street there were more than twenty similar steam-operated corn and oat mills in the town, mainly dotted around the lower part of Newcastle[4]. Now with a population of more than 120,000, the demand for flour to feed its hungry mouths, and oats to help nourish the increasing number of horses employed in the carriage trade[5], was expanding daily. With the mill's increased prosperity Hunter's Terrace became unable to fulfil his father's gentlemanly pretensions, and by the time Slater was 20, the family had moved out to a large detached property in Bulman Village (Gosforth), just north of Newcastle.

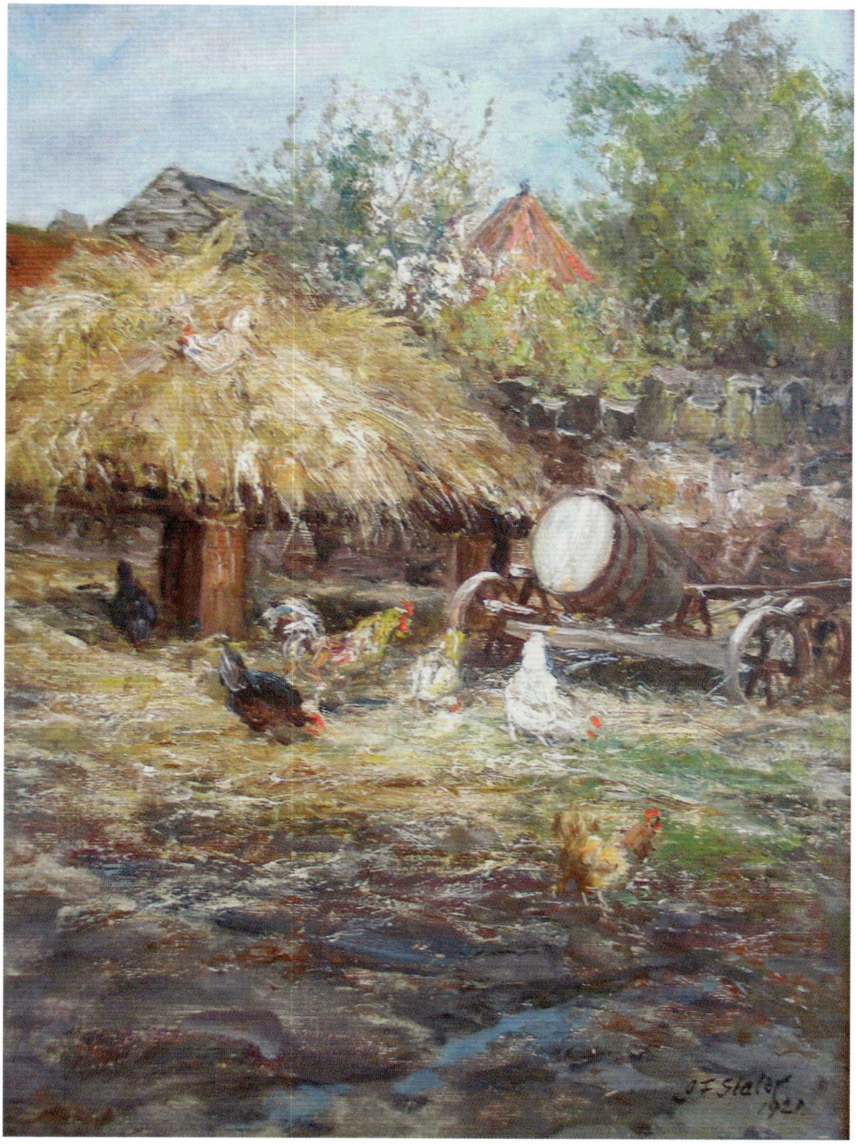

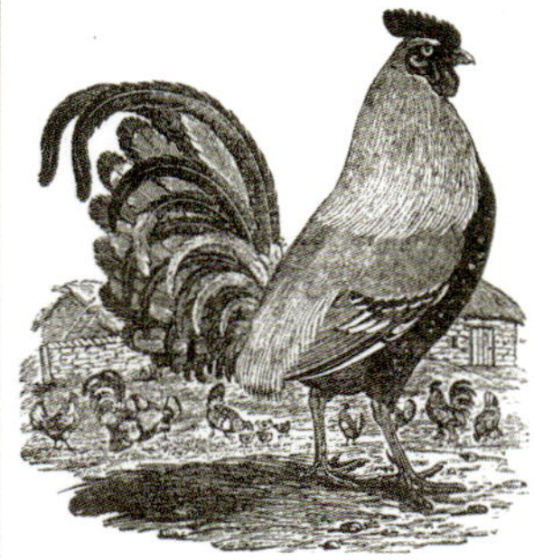

Slater's boyhood fascination with English gamecocks was later in his artistic work extended to domestic poultry generally. This oil of a farmyard near his home at Cullercoats is one of only dozens of examples of this fascination, and one shown by Thomas Bewick in picturing The Cock, above, in his Land Birds book, and many of his vignettes.

This move was to provide Slater with his first taste of rural living, and he could not have been more pleased with the opportunities it presented to explore the fields and woods which then surrounded the family's home in the village. Meanwhile, and in contrast to his sense of freedom while living in the village, his daily work routine had become increasingly onerous. This consisted when he eventually became bookkeeper at the mill, of recording the deliveries from local farms of their grain and oats for milling. Then, when they had been processed, similarly recording the collection of the milled product by clients ranging from food merchants, to stable operators needing forage for their horses. It was exacting, tiring work, and increasingly boring to a young man like him – which perhaps explains what happened next…

Wanderlust

Chapter Two

Shortly before his 21st birthday, having long thought about his plans for the future, Slater surprised his family by announcing that he intended to leave the family business and seek his fortune abroad. Several of his acquaintances in the town had already taken this step and by all accounts done well for themselves. But where to go?

Australia might have seemed an obvious choice. His artist uncle Thomas Flintoff (1809-1891)[6] had left Newcastle around 1850, and after travelling the United States had long been settled in Melbourne. Free emigration to Australia was also available and had been advertised in the *Newcastle Journal*. But although both Australia and Canada figured in his early thinking it was South Africa's most southerly province he plumped for, and with eye-opening results.

Port Elizabeth in the southeast of Cape Province became his destination, and arriving there by ship from Britain in September 1878 he was fortunate to be offered a position as a customs officer in the town soon afterwards. And here he might have remained indefinitely had he not bumped into a fellow Tynesider who put an attractive proposition to him.

Diamonds had recently been found near Jagersfontein, in the Orange Free State, north of Port Elizabeth. Why didn't they set up a store to meet the needs of the prospectors who reportedly were flooding into the area? The idea appealed to Slater, and pooling their savings

The Town Hall and Market Square, Port Elizabeth, in 1874, four years before Slater's arrival.

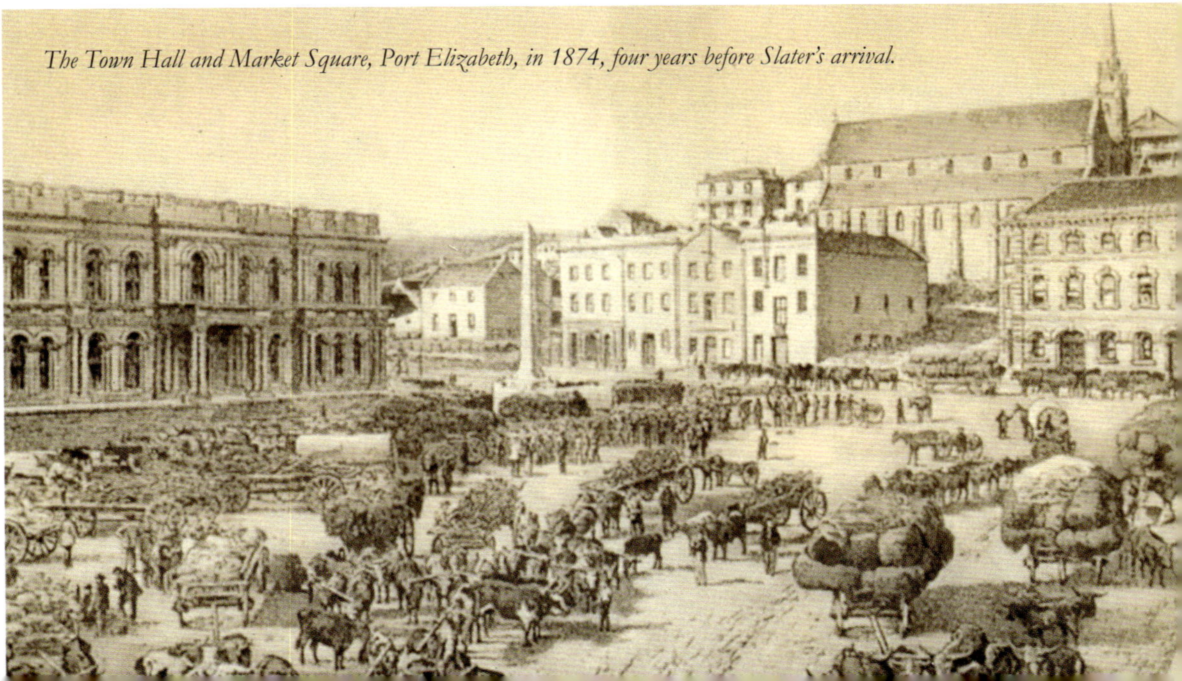

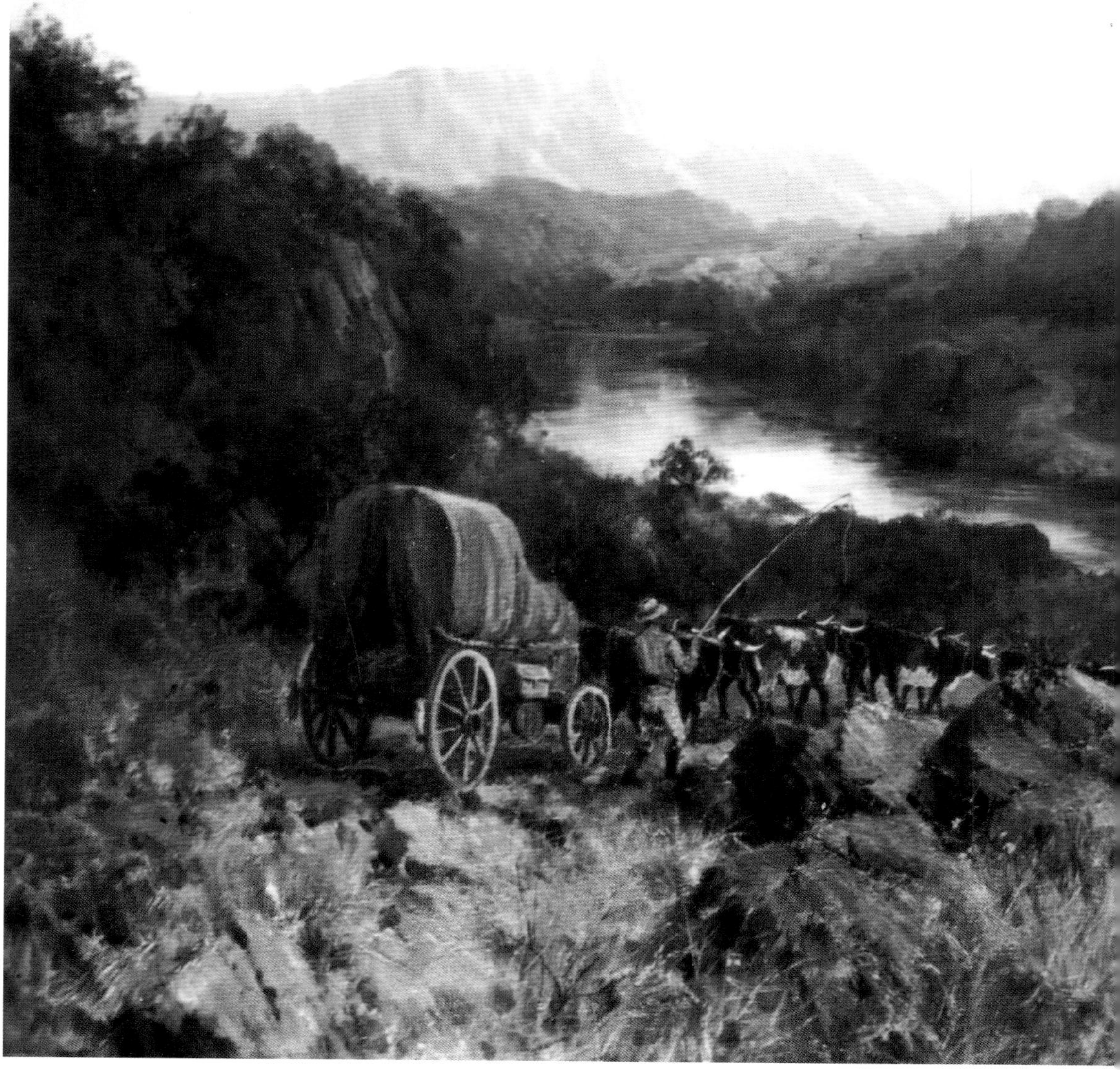

they set off to Jagersfontein and were soon in business. Reports of their time there vary, by one account it was a travelling store drawn by bullocks, another implies that it was a timber building in the middle of the diamond fields. Whatever its character, for some time the venture went well until disaster struck in the form of a freak thunderstorm which ruined their stock. The partnership was dissolved and Slater returned to Britain.

By the beginning of 1881 he had joined the family at its newly purchased home at Stone Villa, Forest Hall, just north of Newcastle. His father had retired there having disposed of the family business and purchased the house from the proceeds. There was, therefore, no prospect of

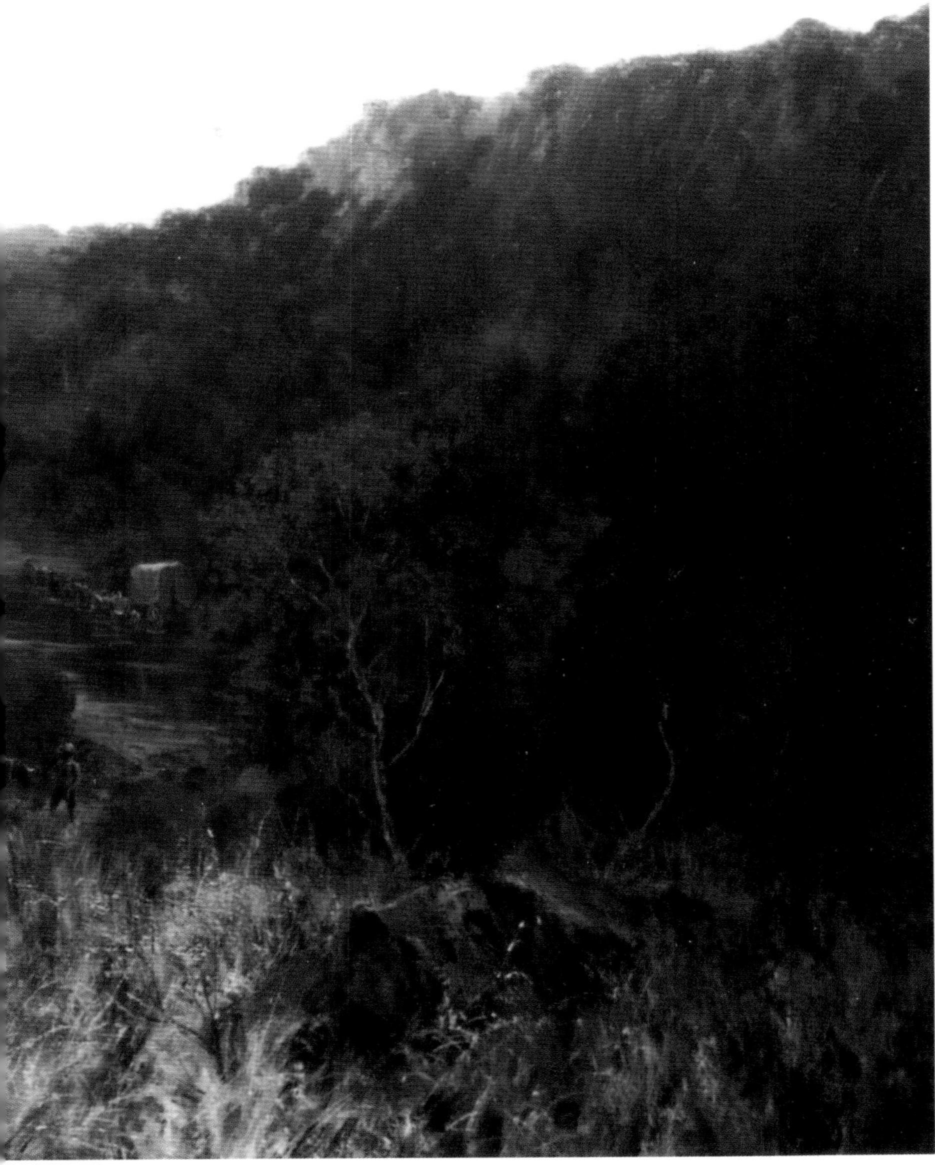

Evening, a view in South Africa, one of the several oils Slater painted on his return to Newcastle recalling his impressions of the country. (Parker Gallery, London)

Slater resuming his former role of company bookkeeper – or managing the business – but in any event he had set his sights on another destination to satisfy his wanderlust: Canada.

Like another British colony Australia, Canada was anxious to attract settlers from England, Scotland and Ireland to help develop its hinterland, and improve its prosperity. Land was cheap and most of it ripe for cultivation and, while his main interest would be farming, there was also the prospect of striking it rich should gold be discovered in the process.

According to family accounts it was his mother who persuaded him otherwise. Sitting together

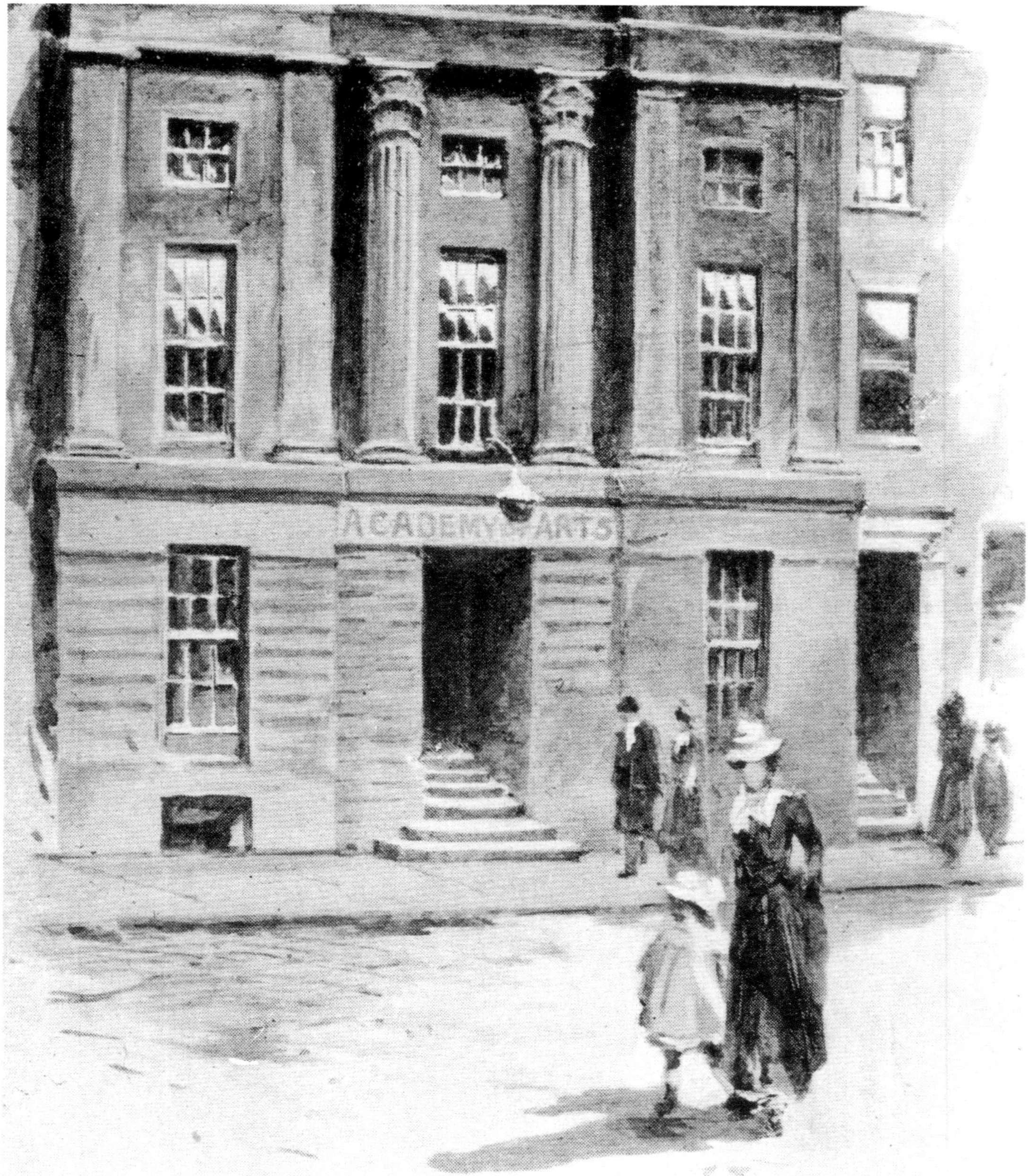

The Academy of Arts, Blackett Street, Newcastle, venue of the 1900 War Fund Exhibition, as later painted by city artist Robert Jobling (1841-1923).

in the living room of Stone Villa she pulled from a folder some of his childhood drawings, pointing out that at even this early stage they were quite as good as her own adult productions. Why go to Canada to farm when he could, perhaps, succeed in becoming a professional artist here in Britain? His sister, Edith Maud, was also gifted artistically[7] and between them they persuaded a man who might otherwise have ended up farming in Canada to become one of the most accomplished artists the North East of England has ever produced.

Slater's South African sojourn was to have a lifelong effect on him both as artist and man. Reputedly unbearded before he left Britain, he returned sporting a healthy growth trimmed in the manner of the Boer farmers he had come across while operating the store in the Orange Free State. The broad-brimmed "Wideawake" hats he favoured throughout his subsequent life were similarly attributed to his imitation of the Boer's customary head-dress. He also retained a deep interest in South African affairs – particularly in those pertaining to the ongoing conflict between Boer and British, and more immediately, that which had begun to occur before he left the Orange Free State, culminating in the First Boer War, and the spectacular defeat of the British at the Battle of Majuba Hill on the 27th February, 1881. He later painted several pictures depicting scenes he had encountered in his travels in the country, showing his first at the Bewick Club, Newcastle, in 1885, entitled *Conveyor's Encampment, Moonlight, South Africa*, and the scene illustrated on pages 18 and 19.

Possibly his best-known work relating to South Africa, however, was his *Majuba Reversed* [8], a celebration of one of Britain's several victories over the Boers before their eventual overthrow by the turn of the century. This epic work was purchased by Andrew Nichol Dodds, publican of North Shields and Tynemouth, for his Preston (North Shields) home, after it was shown at the Exhibition of the Pictures by Local Artists (Artists' War Fund), held at the Academy of Arts, Blackett Street, Newcastle, in 1900. His opinions on South African affairs, and particularly those related to the Boers, were sought for many years after the signing of their surrender to the British on 31st May 1902.

While Slater is not on record of having said in his later life that, like fellow Newcastle-born artist Charles Napier Hemy (1847-1917), of his journey to and from Australia by ship, the experience of travelling to South Africa and back had promoted a lifelong love of the sea (in Hemy's words: "I can remember it entering my soul: it was imprinted on my mind, and I never forgot it."), this must surely have been the case.

Meanwhile, when Slater was on his way from South Africa someone who, like him, would fall in love with the Cullercoats, in which he was to make his final home many years later, had arrived there from America. His name was Winslow Homer (1836-1910) its effect upon whom in determining his final obsession as an artist he first developed in the village, as we shall see in Chapter Six.

Early Days With The Brush

Chapter Three

Within a year of becoming an artist, Slater had made a name for himself by painting a subject that could not have been more popular. Since 1876, a couple of years before he left for South Africa, *The Newcastle Weekly Chronicle* had been running a club for children named *Uncle Toby's Dicky Bird Society*. Thousands of children enrolled in the Society to enjoy its regularly organised entertainments and to read about its activities in each week's issue[9].

By 1883, when he painted his *Members of the Dicky Bird Society* to show at the Gateshead Fine Art & Industrial Exhibition in the September of that year, approximately 70,000 had already joined. He decided to paint a representative group of these members huddled around the imaginary Uncle Toby. It became the sensation of the exhibition, his large work easily upstaging in public interest that of other and much longer established local artists.

It was to be his first taste of publicly exhibiting his work, and he was so taken with the experience that he resolved to repeat it as soon as possible. The opportunity came in the January of the following year when the newly-formed Bewick Club staged its inaugural exhibition in Joel's auction rooms in the city's Pilgrim Street. Here he joined some 140 other local artists by showing two oils and two watercolours: *Quoit Playing; Green Lane near Killingworth; View near Longbenton*, and *Velvet Beds*.

Loan works by several famous artists of the past were included in the 560 on show and although the event received an only lukewarm response from the press, for Slater it was the beginning of a long

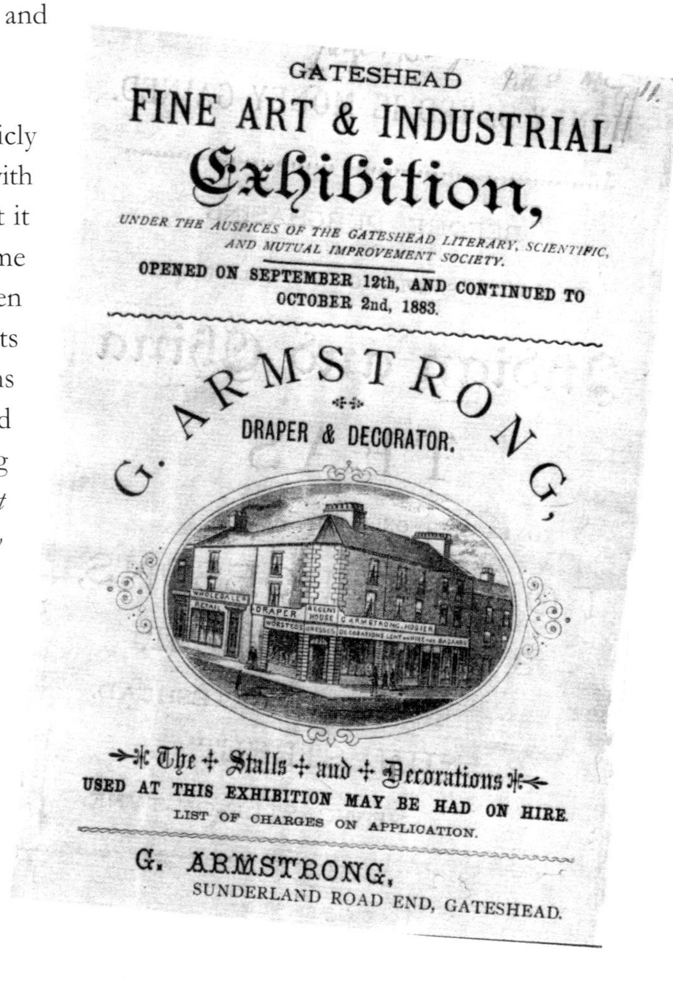

GATESHEAD
FINE ART & INDUSTRIAL
Exhibition,
UNDER THE AUSPICES OF THE GATESHEAD LITERARY, SCIENTIFIC, AND MUTUAL IMPROVEMENT SOCIETY.
OPENED ON SEPTEMBER 12th, AND CONTINUED TO OCTOBER 2nd, 1883.

G. ARMSTRONG,
DRAPER & DECORATOR.

The Stalls and Decorations
USED AT THIS EXHIBITION MAY BE HAD ON HIRE.
LIST OF CHARGES ON APPLICATION.

G. ARMSTRONG,
SUNDERLAND ROAD END, GATESHEAD.

The cover of the Gateshead Fine Art & Industrial Exhibition catalogue.

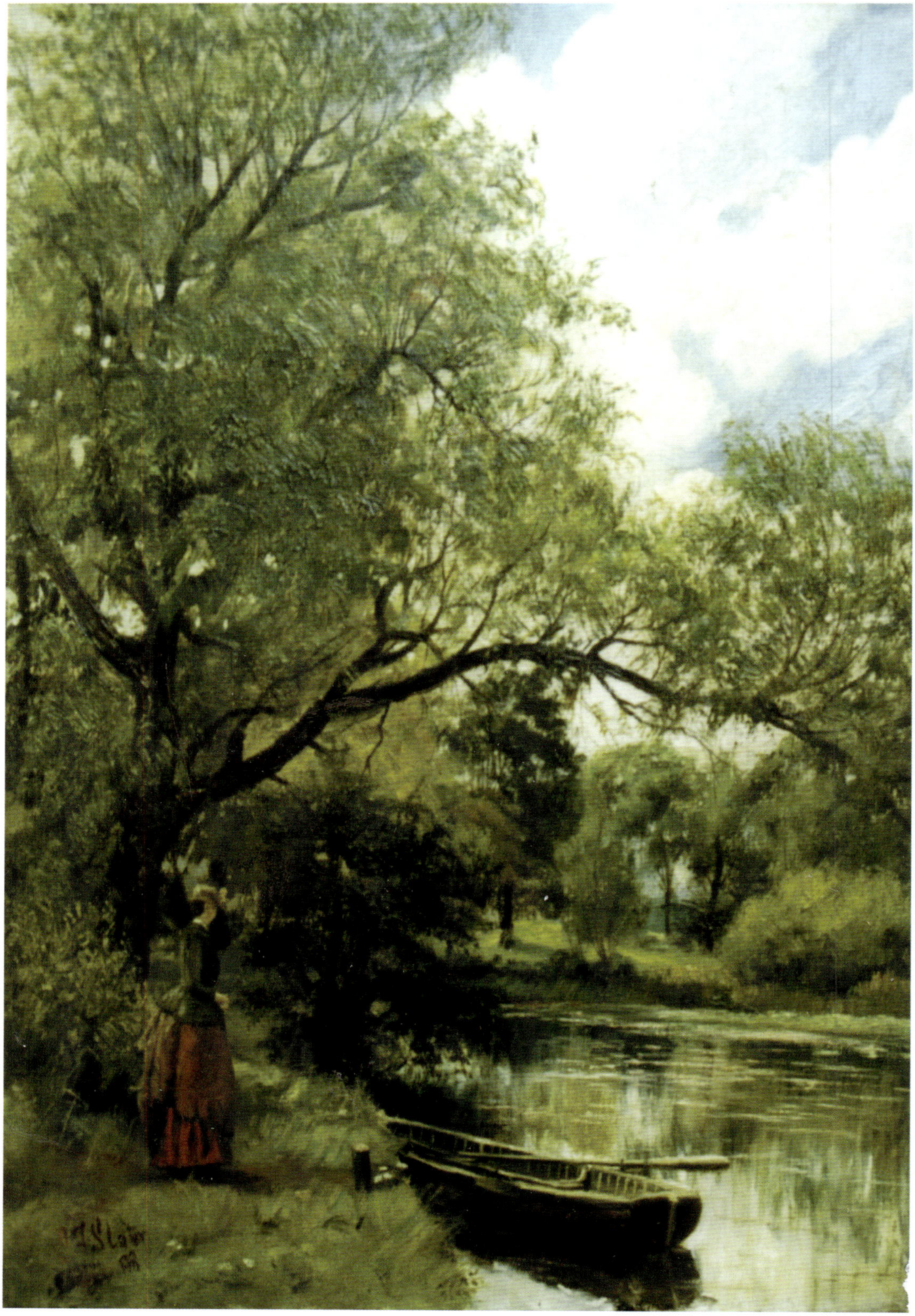

The Boat Landing – Slater's first Royal Academy contribution, of 1889. (Dean Gallery)

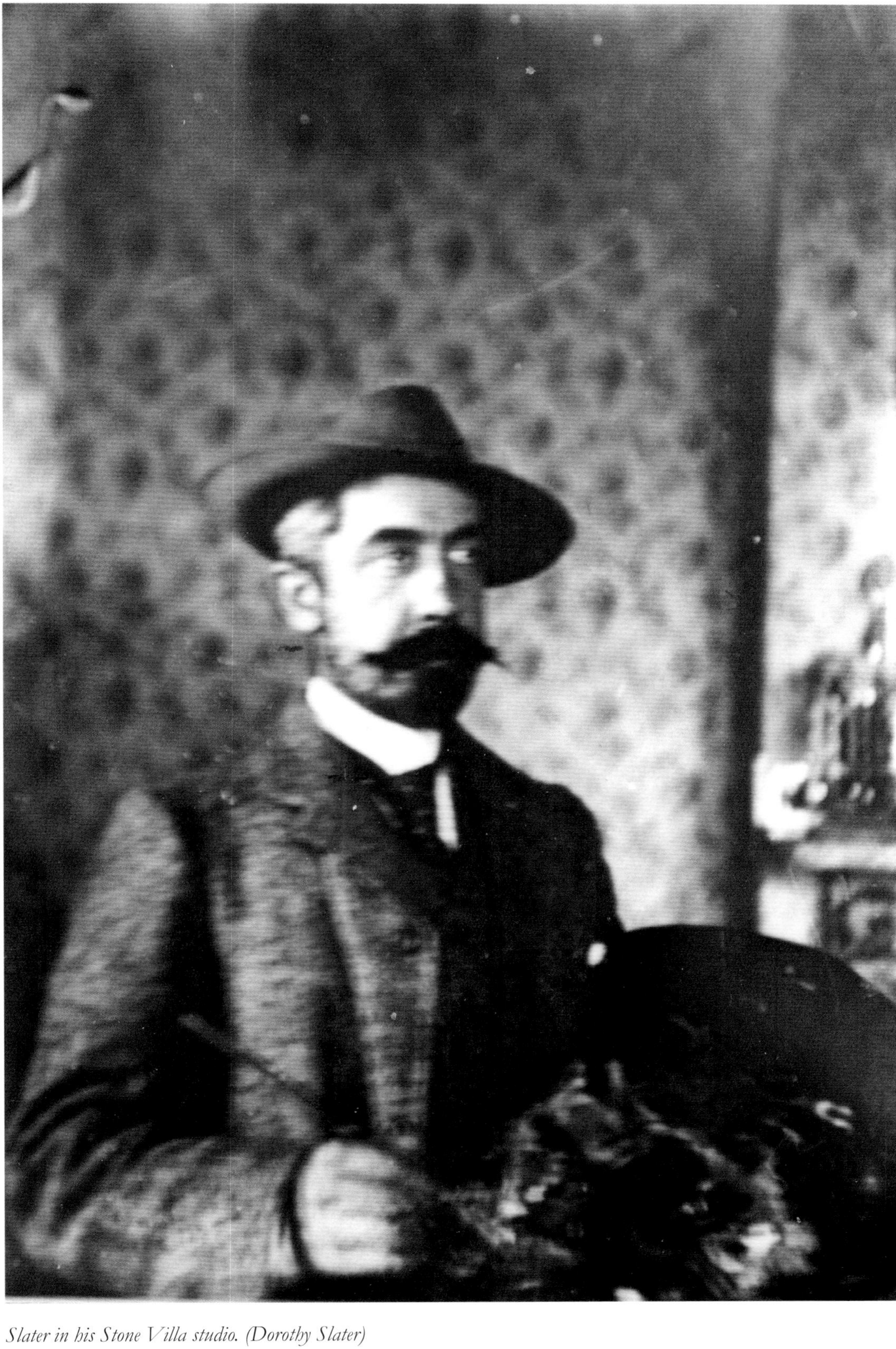

Slater in his Stone Villa studio. (Dorothy Slater)

association with the Club's exhibitions. Meanwhile, while continuing to exhibit with the Club and elsewhere, he sent three of his landscapes to the Royal Mining and Industrial Exhibition held on the so-called Exhibition Park, at Newcastle in 1887: *A Quiet Spot; Springtime near Longbenton*, and *A Hillside near Birtley*. His big breakthrough in exhibition terms, however, came with the acceptance of his landscape *The Boat Landing*, for the Royal Academy Summer Exhibition of 1889, see illustration on page 24.

This small canvas was hung in the 'Gem Room' of the Academy and in the *Newcastle Daily Chronicle* of May 4th, 1889, the art correspondent commented: "In The Boat Landing, Mr J. F. Slater, of Forest Hall, Northumberland, finds a very attractive theme. It consists of a girl beside a skiff with overhanging trees and limpid water, and the hanging committee have shown their appreciation of a piece of good work by giving it a position of importance."

The 'Gem Room' was, of course, a room in the Academy reserved for relatively small but distinctive paintings, and at only 30 x 20ins (66 x 51cms) this certainly qualified in the former respect. That it was also, in the view of the Academy's hanging committee, deemed 'distinctive' must have been very flattering to Slater so early in his career.

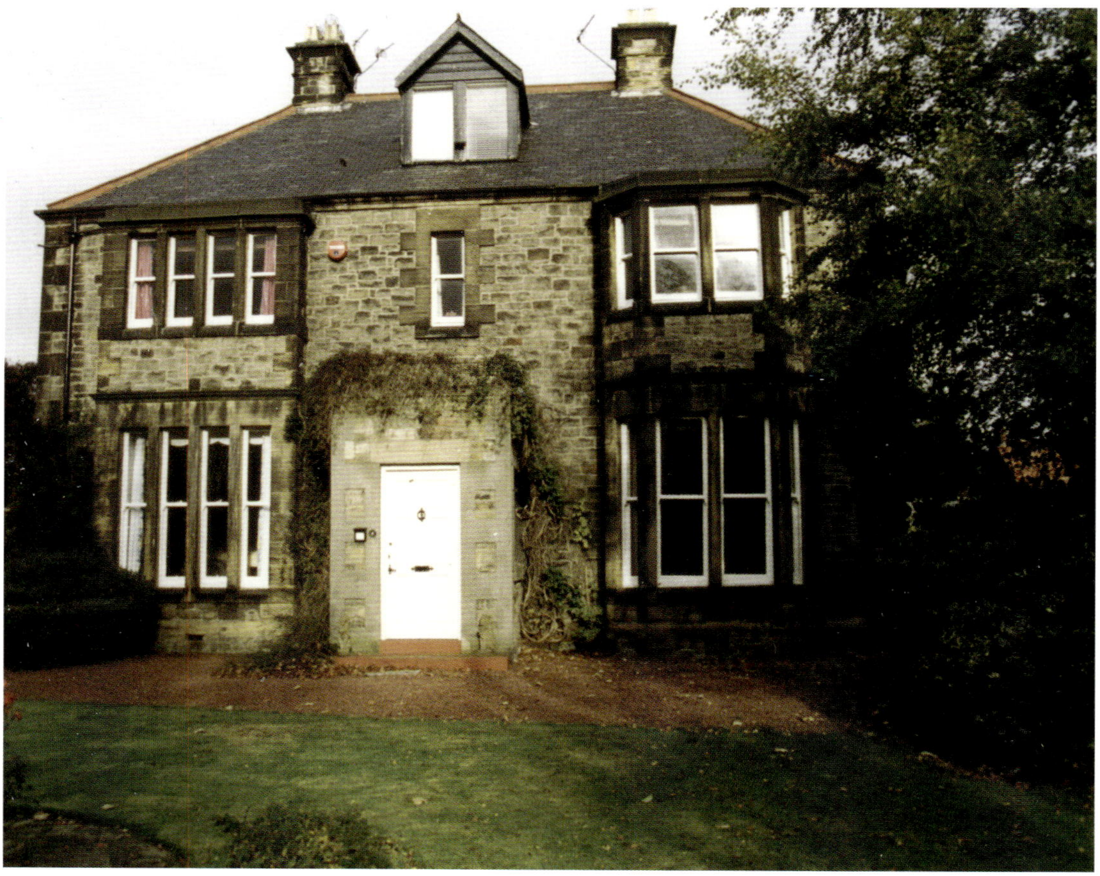

Stone Villa, the Forest Hall family home in which he painted The Boat Landing. (Dr L Cope)

Indeed his excitement, firstly on learning of his painting's acceptance and secondly via the catalogue he received, that it was to be shown in the Academy's 'Gem Room', must have been considerable. The Royal Academy, founded in 1768, was then still Britain's most prestigious art exhibition venue. Each of its annual Summer Exhibitions was privately viewed by the cream of London society – a subject so attractive to British artist William Powell Frith RA (1819-1909) that he painted such an occasion for his 1881 oil *A Private View at the Royal Academy*.

The work by Frith, exhibited at the Academy in 1883, portrayed some of the best-known figures of the day – Gladstone leading the politicians, Leighton and Millais the current Academicians, Oscar Wilde among the aesthetes, Lily Langtry and Ellen Terry the beauties. Those who attended the Private View of the 1889 show in which Slater's *The Boat Landing* was shown were presumably composed of the same mix of society figures.

Although the press comment about its showing at the Academy was brief, it inspired Slater to start an album of cuttings of such comments which he would maintain throughout his subsequent career as an artist. And in this respect he demonstrated a then unusual awareness of the value of receiving press comment about his work and its deployment in its printed form in further promoting his career. His progressively burgeoning folder of cuttings would always find a prominent place in his later studios for prospective clients to browse through while waiting to collect their purchases and encourage them to make more.

Such cuttings alluding to his first and subsequently 21 Royal Academy Exhibition acceptances over the years were, of course, particularly welcome additions to his collection, apart from those referring to the many other exhibitions in which he participated.

By the time Slater began exhibiting at the Academy, some 10,000 works were being submitted to the hanging committee each year of which only 10% were eventually hung, those at eye level described as "on the line" (see next chapter for reference); those hung close to gallery's ceilings "skied".

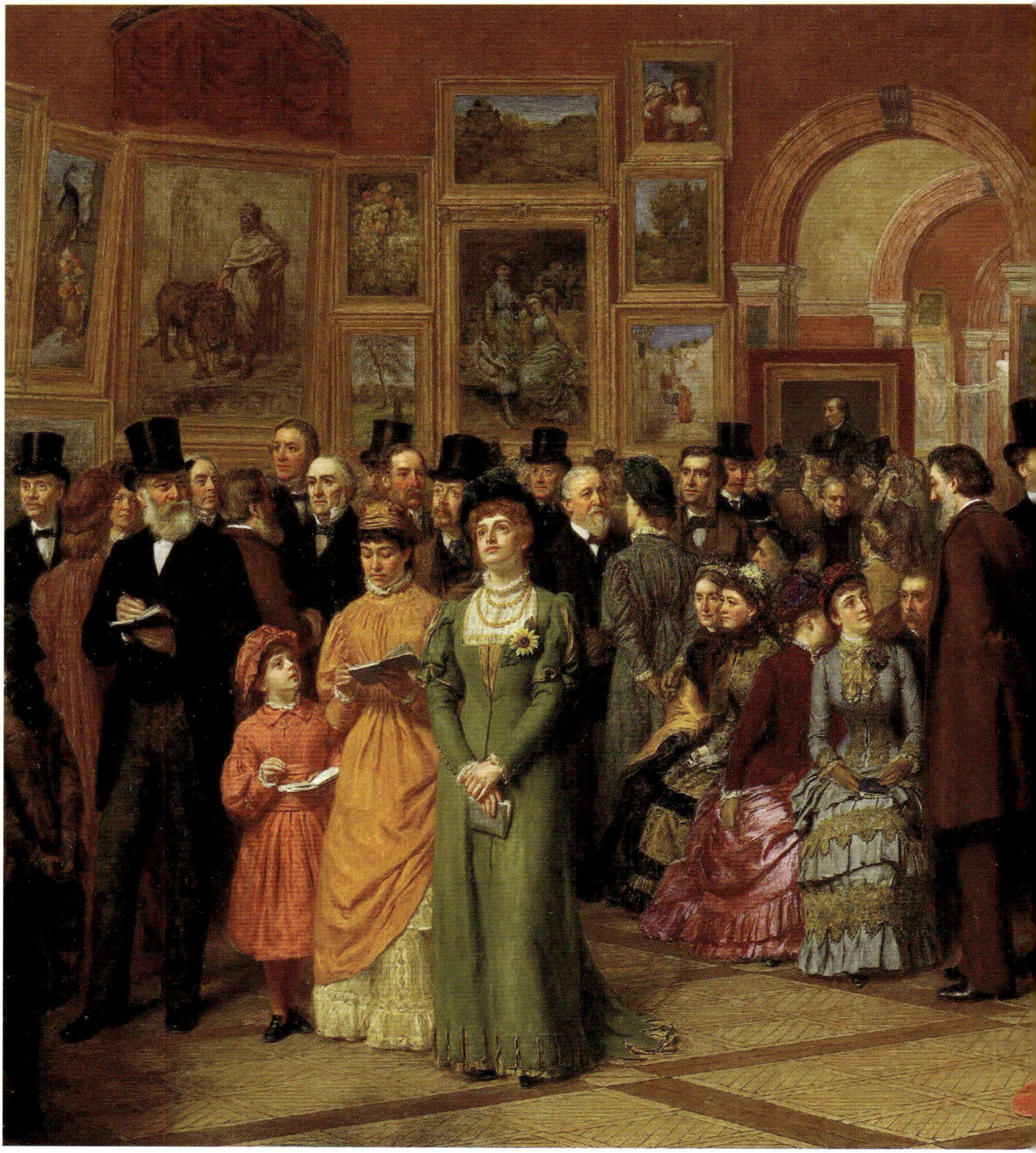

Frith's 1881 oil, The Private View at the Royal Academy. (Private collection)

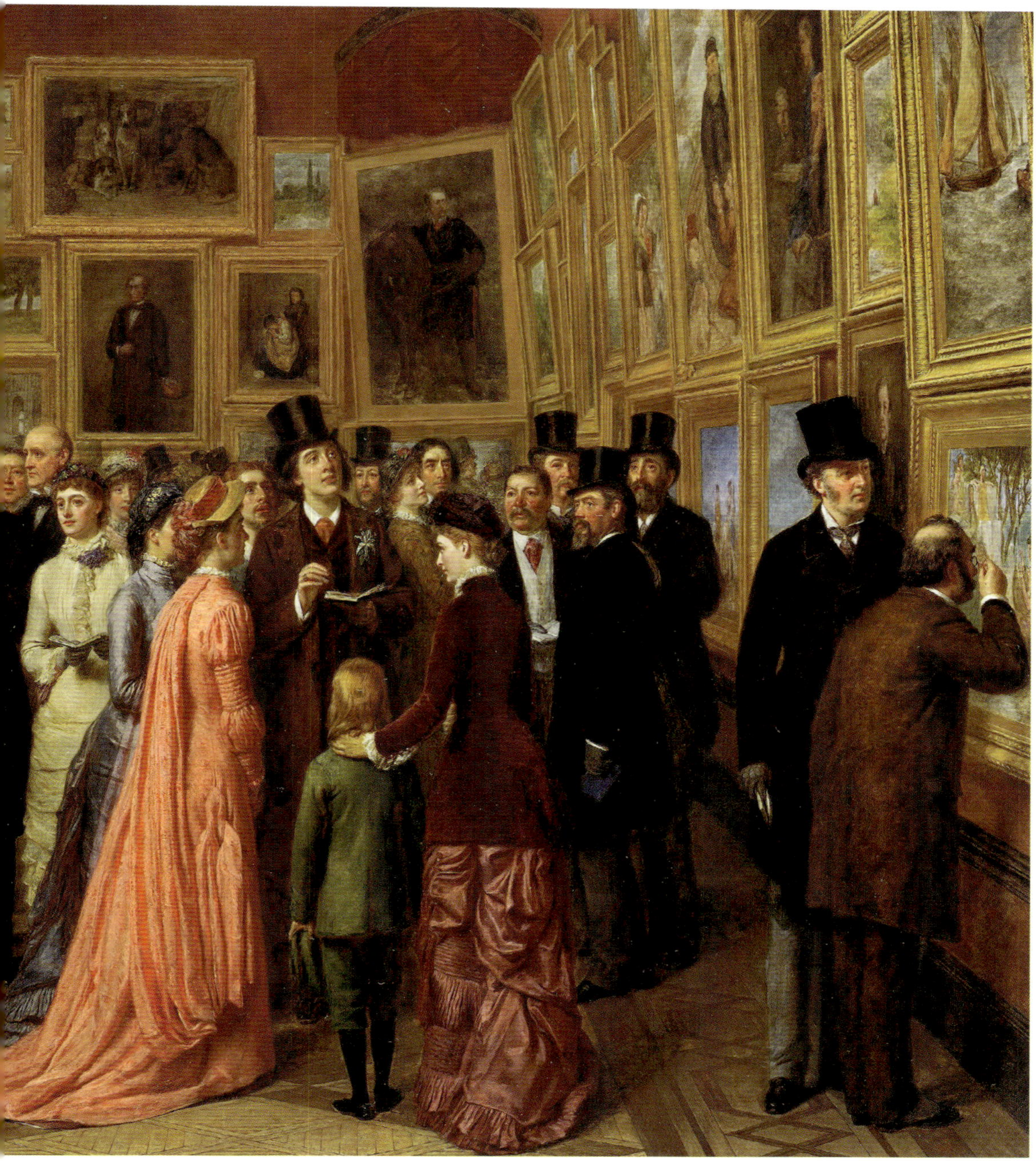

His First City Studio

Chapter Four

Slater had continued to live with his family at Stone Villa throughout his early years as an artist, using an upper-floor bedroom as his studio. But following the showing of his third exhibit at the Royal Academy in 1892 – *Going to Market* – he became increasingly anxious to establish a studio in Newcastle.

The location he chose was in the city's Mosley Street, just near its junction with Pilgrim Street. Established at No.13 by 1894[10], in what was part of Mawson's Building, he staged his first private exhibition of his work, and ran into its first criticism.

"My first studio was in a quiet neighbourhood," he was to recall some years later in his *Odds & Ends from an Artist's Note Book*, of 1914. "It was approached from a private flight of steps leading to the door. I remember how carefully I furnished it with all that would make it attractive, not even forgetting curtains and other upholstery, also a chic tea-set to entertain visitors to tea.

"I was not long while there, but during my stay I began to learn the opinions of other people. I held a small exhibition of my work and sent out invitations, and among those who visited me was one to whom I showed my Royal Academy picture of that year. He looked at it and remarked: 'It is not finished!' I asked, 'Where?' and, drawing my attention to a certain part he affirmed: 'Yes, that is not finished.' My next query was: 'Would it surprise you to know that the picture had been on the line at the Royal Academy?'

"He was evidently at a loss to understand how it could have been selected, and chose for himself a picture from my collection which he thought thoroughly finished, and no doubt it was, for there was nothing whatever left to the imagination!"

At this point it might be appropriate to take stock of Slater's work as an artist to date. He was supported by his father in his early years, and therefore arguably classifiable as an 'amateur'. But he had developed remarkably swiftly as a painter by the time he opened his first city studio. Indeed, having shown his work publicly two years after his return from South Africa, and made his debut at the Royal Academy within eight years, his development might have been deemed spectacular.

Without academic or any other formal type of training he had achieved this (and the success

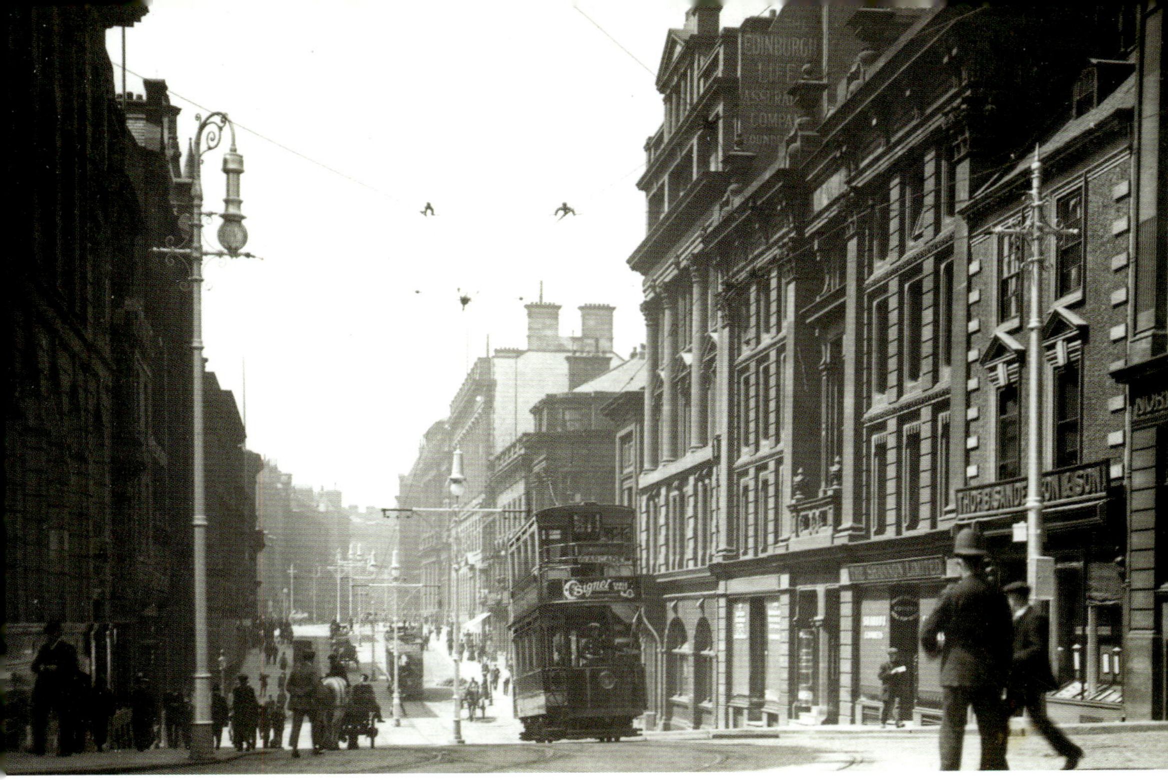

Mosley Street, Newcastle, c.1900. No.13, in which he set up his first city studio, is on the right.

in selling his work that followed) in competition with other locally-based artists who had attended either the Government School of Design in Newcastle, or other teaching facilities. Most important is the fact that being largely self taught he had developed a personal style which, although at this stage he was oblivious, closely approximated that which was being developed in France by artists who were quickly dubbed 'Impressionists'. The incident in his studio recounted earlier is, therefore, significant beyond the status of mere anecdote in anticipating his eventual entitlement to be regarded as one of Britain's earlier practitioners of Impressionism, little as this has been recognised to date. He understandably had to continue painting pictures following prevailing contemporary taste of the sort chosen from his first city studio exhibition by his critical visitor, but the one which was criticised indicates where his main stylistic interests lay.

But then, as art expert Philip Hook, in his book *Breakfast at Sotheby's*, 2013, remarks, in paraphrasing an observation by American novelist and Anglophile Henry James regarding the difference between the French and English attitudes to art at that time: "One of the reasons why Impressionism failed to catch on immediately in England was that the English thought it lazy. Why should we give good money for something that didn't take very long to knock up?"

Slater, like many other British artists of the day remained acutely aware of the financial penalties of succumbing entirely to the allure of Impressionism, which is why he continued to the end to paint works very much in the taste of a previous era, and it is, perhaps, significant

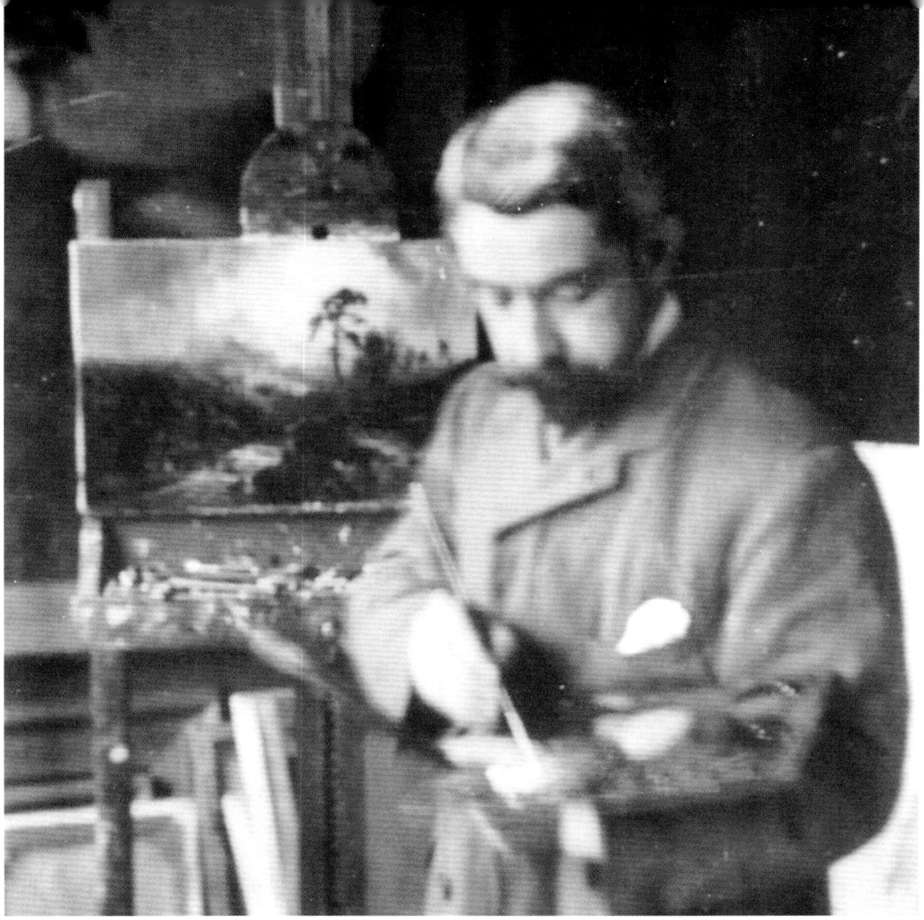

Painting in his first city studio. (Dorothy Slater)

that the majority of the dozens of unsold works remaining in his Cullercoats studio on his death were broadly Impressionist in style (see "Aftermath" chapter). The English reserve remarked previously in regard to these had persisted (admittedly on a progressively reducing scale) for several decades after it had evaporated in France and elsewhere on the Continent.

Whatever pressures Slater might have felt under to sell his work at this early stage in his career, these were increased as a consequence of one of his first and subsequently rare professional visits to Westmorland, and the adjacent Lake District, to paint. In late 1896 he was painting a landscape just outside Kendal, when, according to family legend, he suddenly became aware that he was being secretly watched by an attractive young woman. They struck up a conversation and, after noting where she lived, he later wrote to her asking if they could meet again. She was Sarah Ann Atkinson, the fourth daughter of Thomas Martindale Atkinson, a tenant farmer at Burneside, near Kendal, and after a brief courtship the couple married at the Baptist Chapel, Howard Street, North Shields, on 28th April, 1898.

To finance their honeymoon at Grindleford, Derbyshire,[11] and eventually setting up home with Sarah, he took the bold step of holding a public exhibition of his work at Davison's Gallery, in the Academy of Arts, Blackett Street, Newcastle, in January of that year. He

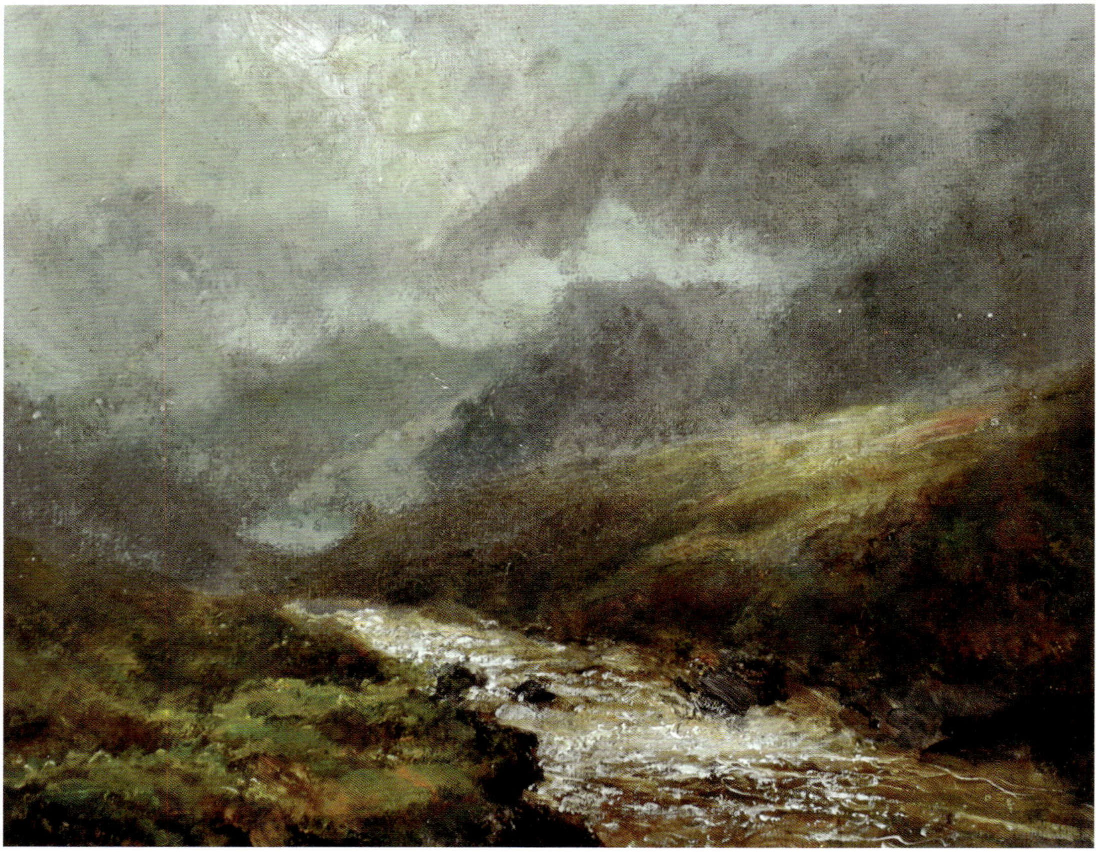

A typical Scottish scene painted on one of his annual trips until age curtailed them in the 1920s. (Anderson & Garland)

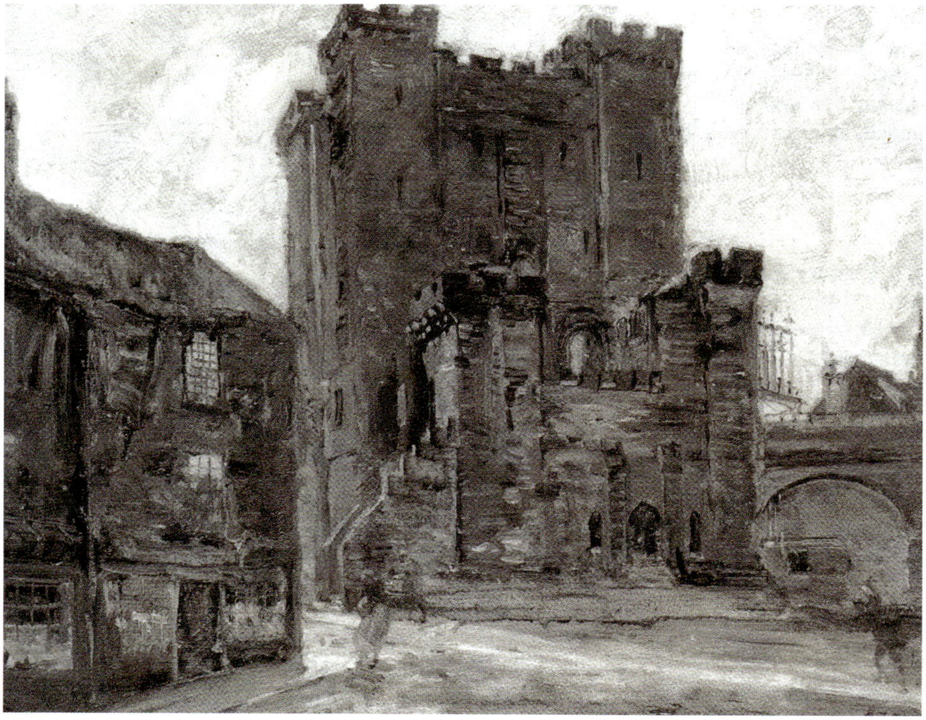

Newcastle Keep, one of the few Newcastle historic landmarks Slater chose to paint, along with St Nicholas's Cathedral. (Anderson & Garland)

followed this with a second show there on his return, on 10th June 1898. This second show netted him about £180, and either with, or without Sarah, he immediately set out on what had become a regular event for several years – a painting trip to Scotland.

These Scottish trips were to produce dozens of works portraying un-named Highland Glens, usually in Eastern Scotland, wreathed in mist or falling rain. None, or very few, ever included any hint of the human presence, perhaps because - like his pure seascapes - he wanted to express in them their raw, natural character - a character he is on record as saying he found in many of the scenes he encountered when crossing the Veldt during his period in South Africa.

In treating his Scottish landscapes as he did, he wanted to express this feeling of raw nature, not prettifying them in the process, as so many other artists did, on the back of Victoria and Albert's sentimental preference for scenes showing peasants, shepherds, ferrymen and gamekeepers about their everyday work. These he left to the works of fellow North East artists like George Blackie Sticks (1843-1900), Edward Train (1801-1866), and Duncan Fraser McLea (1841-1916). Or was it simply that, in contrast to these three accomplished artists, he wanted his paintings to appeal to their potential purchasers because they would feel as they looked at them on their walls on cold winter nights a sense of comfortable detachment from their implied bleakness and inhospitality? Whatever his reasons for selecting and treating his Scottish subjects as he did, Slater is only on record as showing any works relating to the area, in Scotland itself on one occasion, and these not remotely like his usual ones; these were his *Steeple from Mooran House Garden*, and the other, *Montrose Basin,* shown at the Montrose Art Exhibition in 1929. The remaining work, titled *Sunshine & Shade*, had no apparent connection with Scotland and had already been shown in Newcastle before its purchase by its lender to the exhibition. This was, however, not his first venture into exhibiting in Scotland. In 1920 he showed one of his typical poultry scenes at the Royal Scottish Academy.

Of course, Slater's landscape work did not consist only of Scottish scenes, the demand for local ones could not be ignored. So, among several more local destinations to paint, were the Tyne Valley, North Tyne Valley, South Tyne Valley, Coquet Valley, Allen Valley, and North Yorkshire (though not, it would seem, Staithes). As to the period in which these and, indeed, most of his landscape and other works were painted, it is difficult to determine, as he only rarely dated those of his pre-1900 period, and later ones intermittently.

Urban landscapes did not much feature in Slater's work; Newcastle Keep and St Nicholas's Cathedral being exceptions. The latter he found particularly attractive to paint, especially from the top of the former, encompassing the buildings in the foreground. But one such subject to which, he was, perhaps, predictably attracted given his need to visit it to buy his oilskins, was South Shields Market Place, the location at No 5 of Barbour, the area's major suppliers of the garments he wore as a 'Weatherproof Artist', and now a world-famous name.

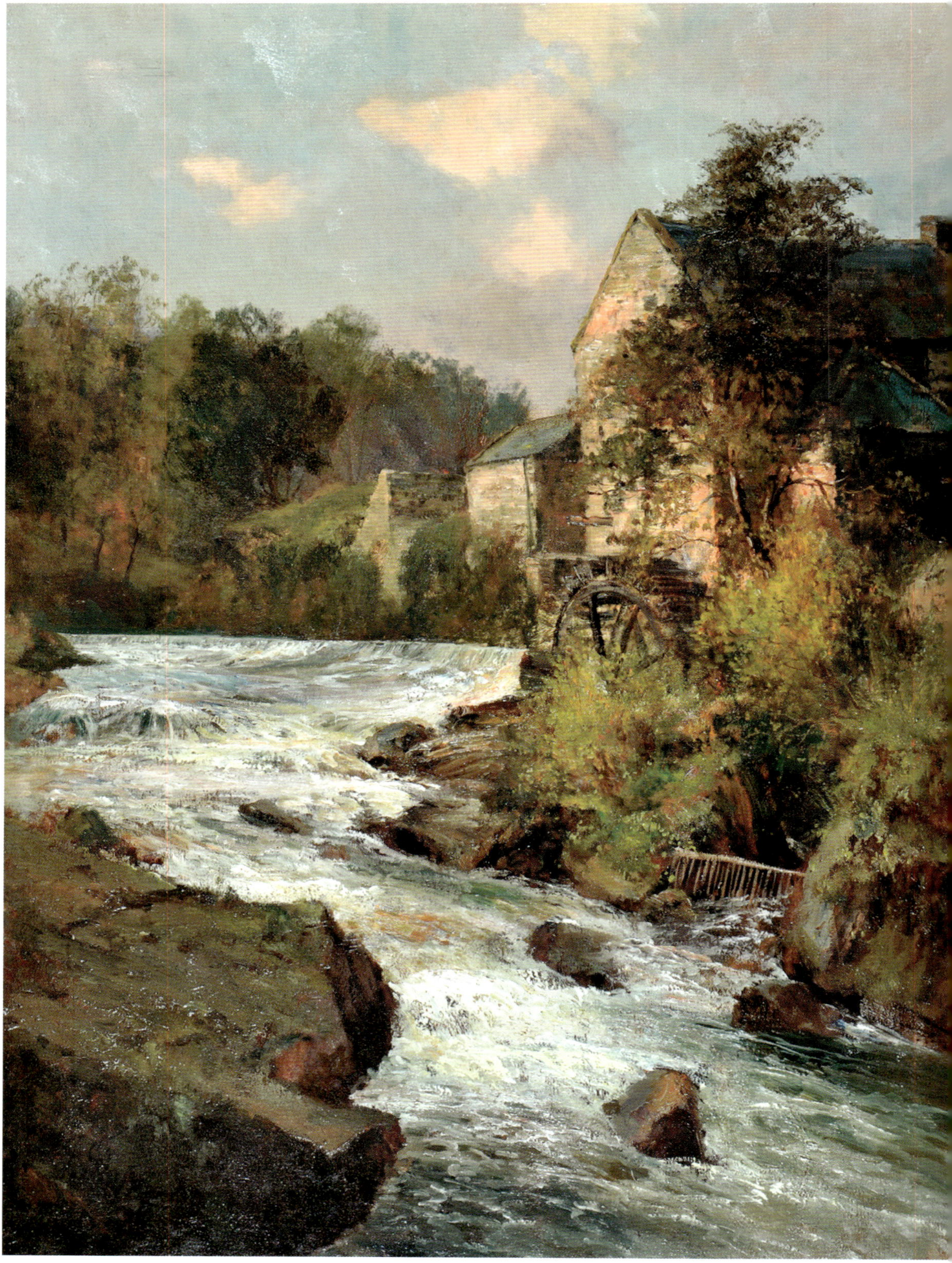

Thrum Mill, Rothbury. (Anderson & Garland)

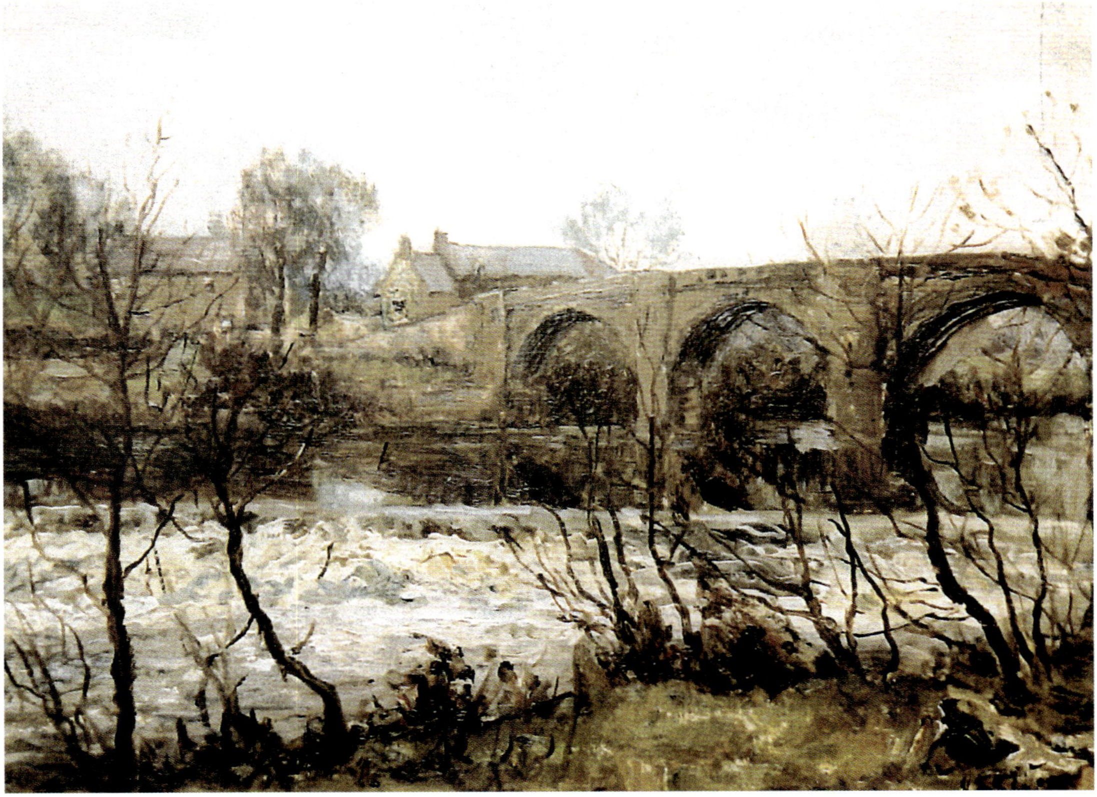

Chollerford Bridge, and the George Inn, on the North Tyne. (Anderson & Garland)

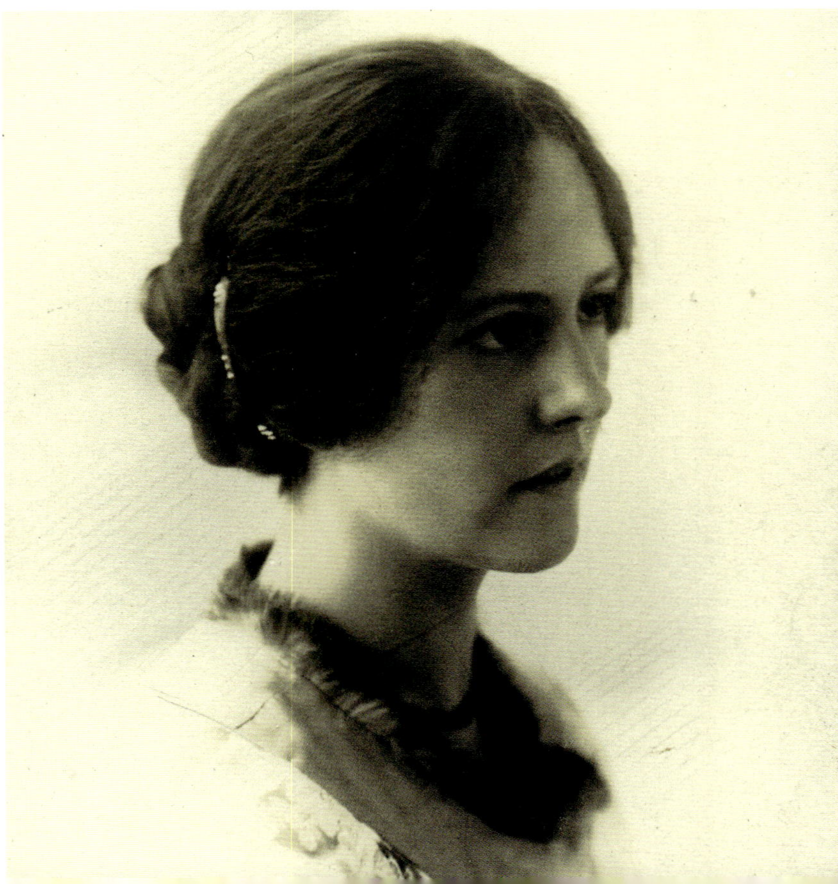

Slater's wife Sarah at about the time they first met. (Dorothy Slater)

The Weatherproof Artist

Chapter Five

By the late 1890s Slater was showing a marked preference for certain types of subject in his exhibited work, portraying the sea in windy weather, or the misty Highland Glens referred to in the previous chapter. This did not go unnoticed by the local press and led to him receiving a nickname by which he would remain known for the rest of his life.

One day, painting in his Mosley Street studio he heard a discreet tap on the door leading to the building's top-floor landing. Forty at the time, and having recently shown some of his typical work at the city's Bewick Club, he opened the door to find himself confronted by a local reporter who said he had come to find out how the artist had earned his reputation as an 'all-weather painter'.

Within a few hours the reporter was sitting at his desk in the offices of the *North Mail* in the city's Westgate Road writing the answer: "Not every artist is sufficiently enthusiastic in his work to paint a picture in the middle of a January snowstorm," he began his piece, "or with a wild north-easter blowing at his back.

"A Mail correspondent discovered such a curiosity recently in the person of a well-known Newcastle artist who paints some of his best pictures in exposed parts of the coast during the winter season – a time when most of us prefer doing our work in a well-warmed room." Slater's explanation of how he coped with the task gave the story its headline – and the nick-name by which he would always later be known: 'I am weather and waterproof from head to foot,' he said, 'that way I can stand the roughest gale.' 'A WEATHERPROOF ARTIST', as the reporter entitled his piece, appeared in *The Mail* on January 9th 1898, and concluded, perhaps unnecessarily, that he was no "milk and water artist".

The first paintings that had established this well-deserved nickname had been executed on expeditions to the coast from his Stone Villa studio, travelling from the local railway station with his easel and brushes perched on his knees. However, unlike most other artists setting out to the coast to paint he chose the windy day in preference to the calm, knowing that he would find the sea lashed into a foaming frenzy along the cliffs.

In *Odds & Ends from an Artist's Note Book* (see chapter "His move to the coast") he admits that while these early expeditions resulted in small scale oil sketches that he translated into larger productions back in his studio, he later mastered the technique of painting much larger pictures

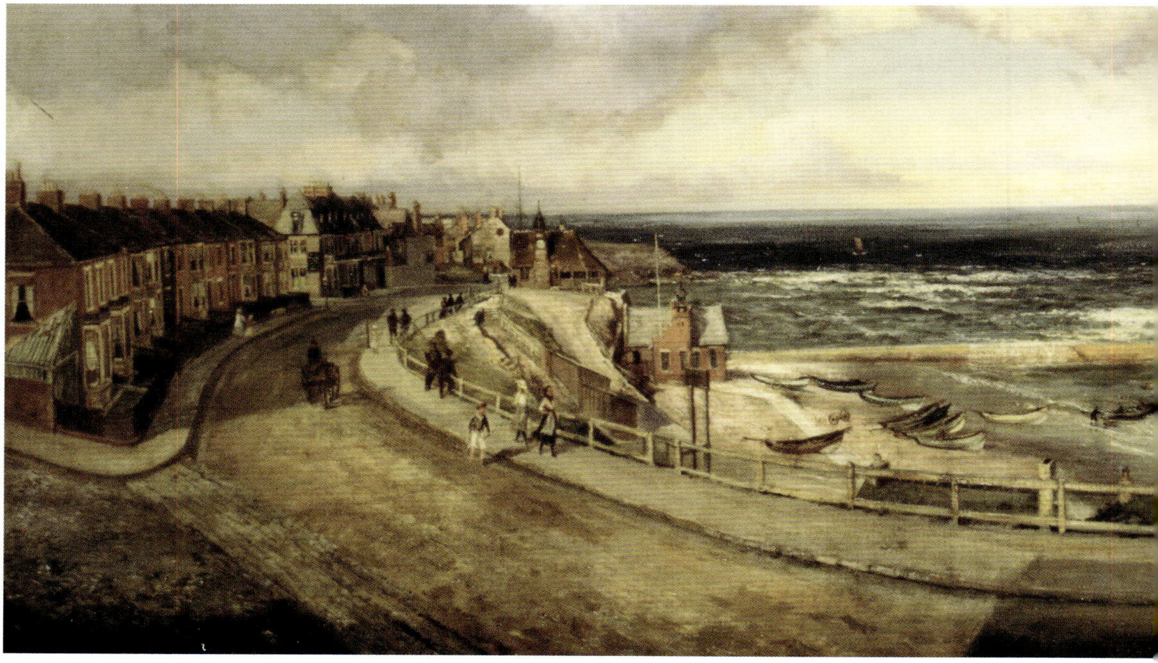

Slater's panoramic view of Cullercoats, painted in 1905. (Anderson & Garland)

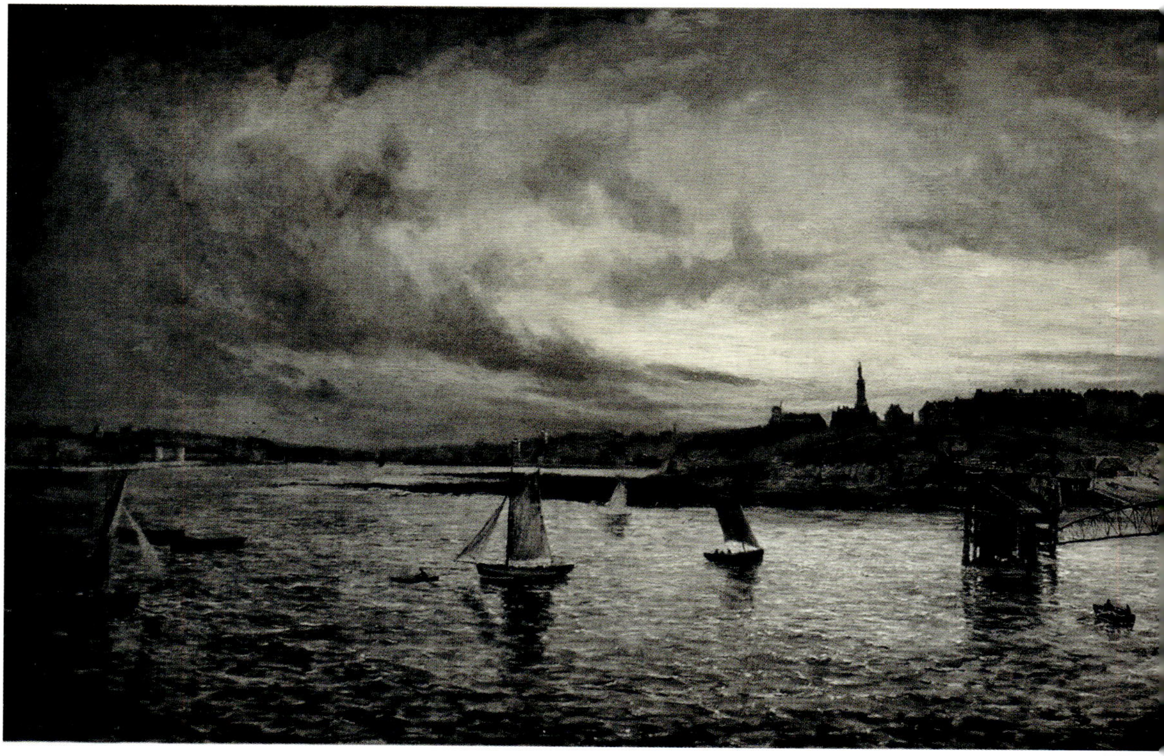

A photogravure of Slater's view of Tynemouth, of 1910 – another popular reproduction of his work – in this case a limited-editi

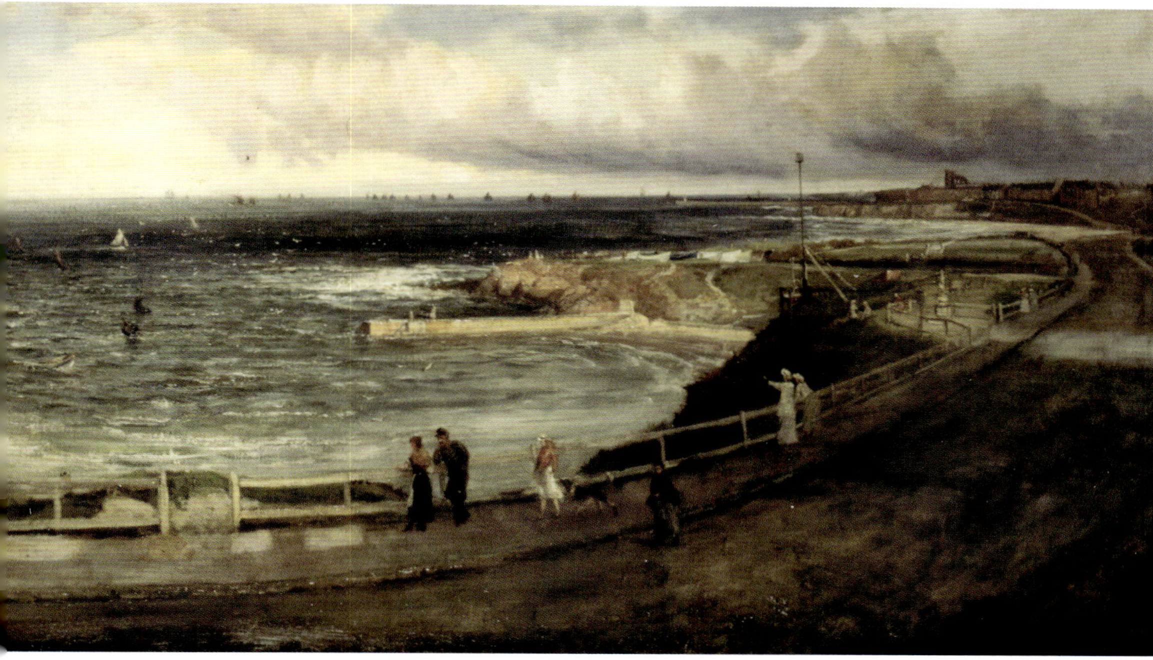

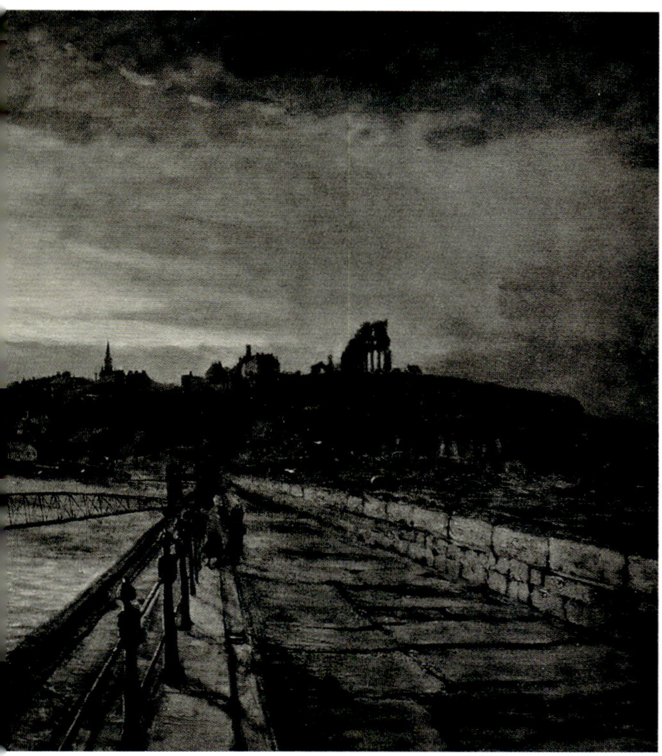

(Anderson & Garland)

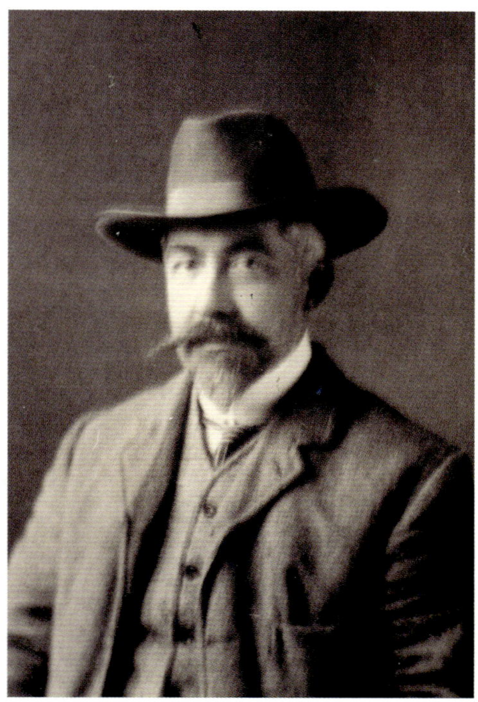

Slater as he looked when he painted his Cullercoats panorama. (Dorothy Slater)

on the spot – but of this more later. The most pressing problem after he had opened his city studio, and was later living at Killingworth, was having to travel to paint his increasingly preferred subject. But how to solve this problem?

By the early years of the new century, and now having moved his studio from 13 Mosley Street, to 54 Pilgrim Street nearby, he was in even more of a dilemma. He had established a good clientele for his work in Newcastle and, with the opening of the Laing Art Gallery in 1904 and its staging by the following year of an excellent new selling medium in its *Artists of the Northern Counties* exhibitions, there was a strong argument for remaining in the city. Further, his family (Mary Bertha, b.1899; Agnes Dorothy, b.1900; Thomas Waldron, b.1902, and John Martindale, b.1904), were happily settled at their home at Woodlands, Killingworth, and his surviving siblings[12] were still living nearby following the death of their father in 1896, and their mother in 1901.

It was, perhaps, the success of one of his largest and most ambitious paintings of the coast, executed in 1905, which determined him eventually to move, and, ironically, it was far in treatment from his earlier and later coastal productions. Sketched from the first-floor balcony of a property at the northern end of Beverley Terrace in Cullercoats and painted at his city studio, it shows a detailed panoramic view of the village from the east, encompassing distant Tynemouth Priory and Castle, and resulted not only in an oil measuring a staggering 8ft 4ins (254cms) wide, but a photogravure print, which, in either monochrome, or hand-coloured form, quickly found its way into homes all over the Cullercoats area. Its topographical scope, panoramic as it was, couldn't, however, from the vantage point from which it was sketched, include several of the major manmade landmarks which had been added to the local coastline in recent decades. Starting at the north was the lighthouse built on St Mary's Island in 1897. It was to the south of this feature, however, that other and earlier major additions had been made. The first of these was the Grand Hotel, Tynemouth, of 1872. This was joined by St George's Church, Cullercoats, in 1884 and the so-called Plaza Leisure Centre, Tynemouth, in 1887. With all of these he would become familiar on a daily basis after his move to live on this, his favourite stretch of the North East coast.

Opposite: Table Rocks, Whitley Bay, a more tranquil sea and coastal study painted by Slater. (Anderson & Garland)

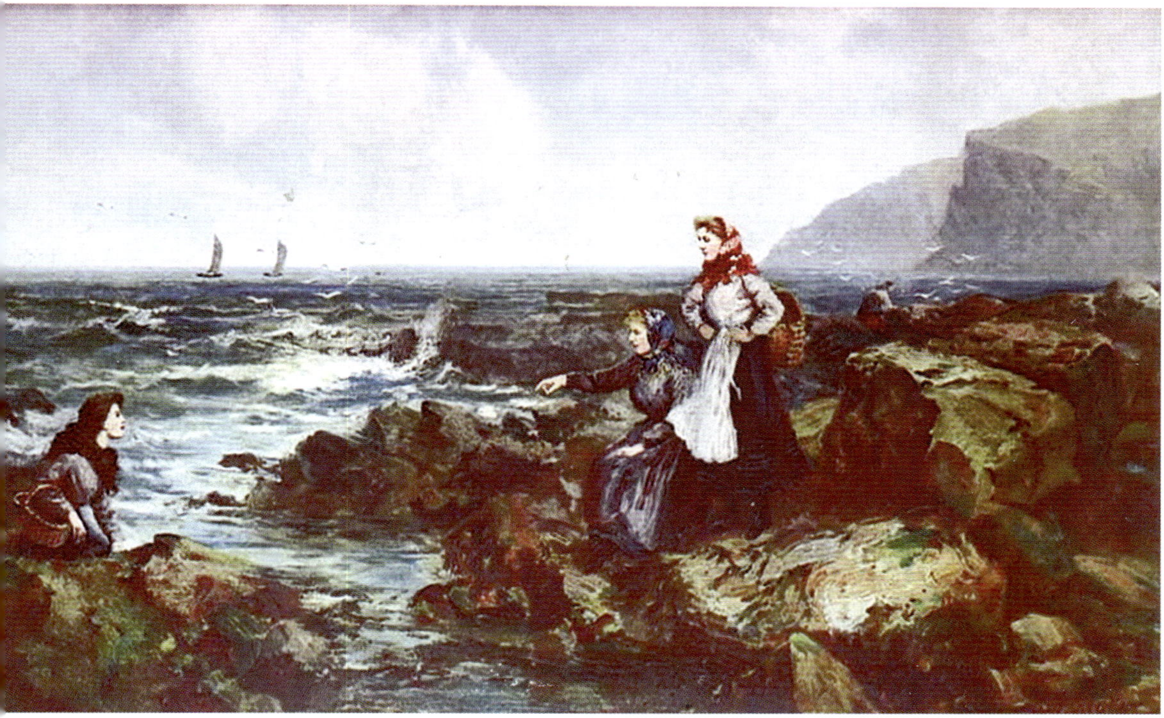

Cullercoats Fishergirls, another example of Slater's work reproduced as a print. (Anderson & Garland)

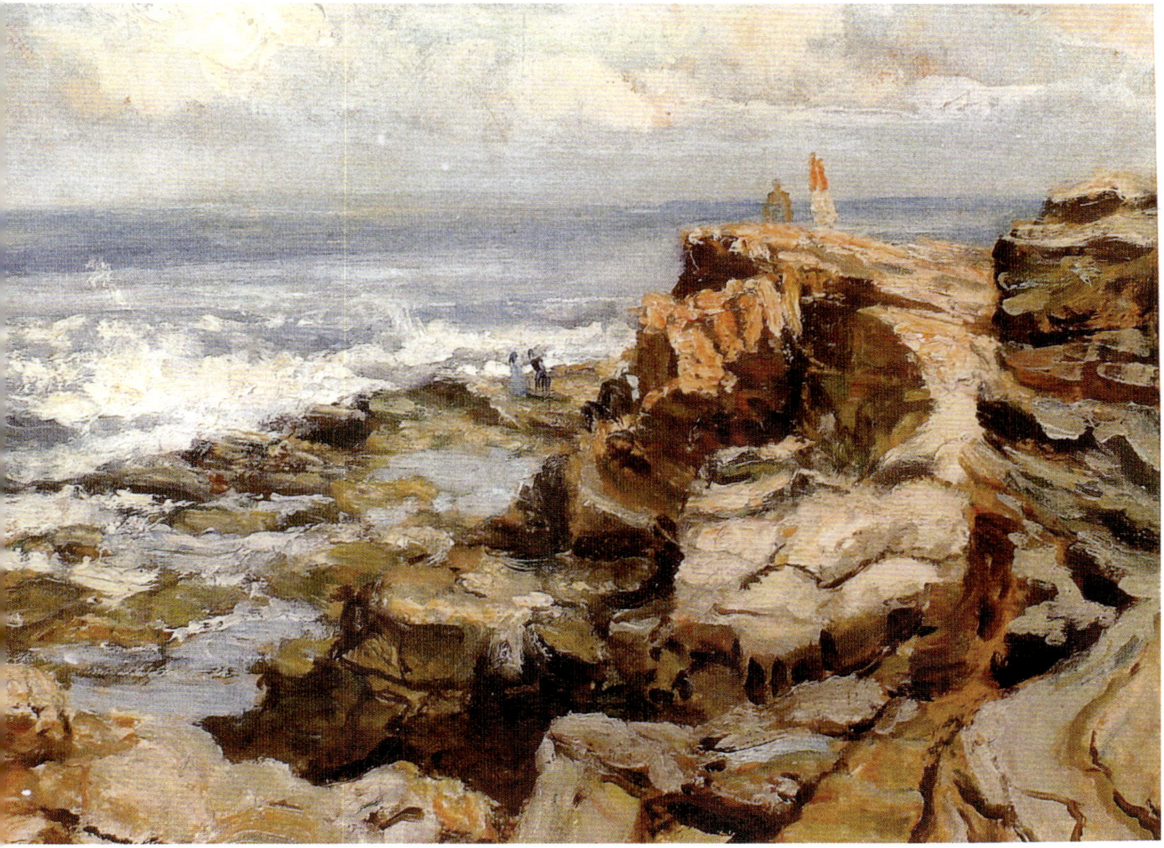

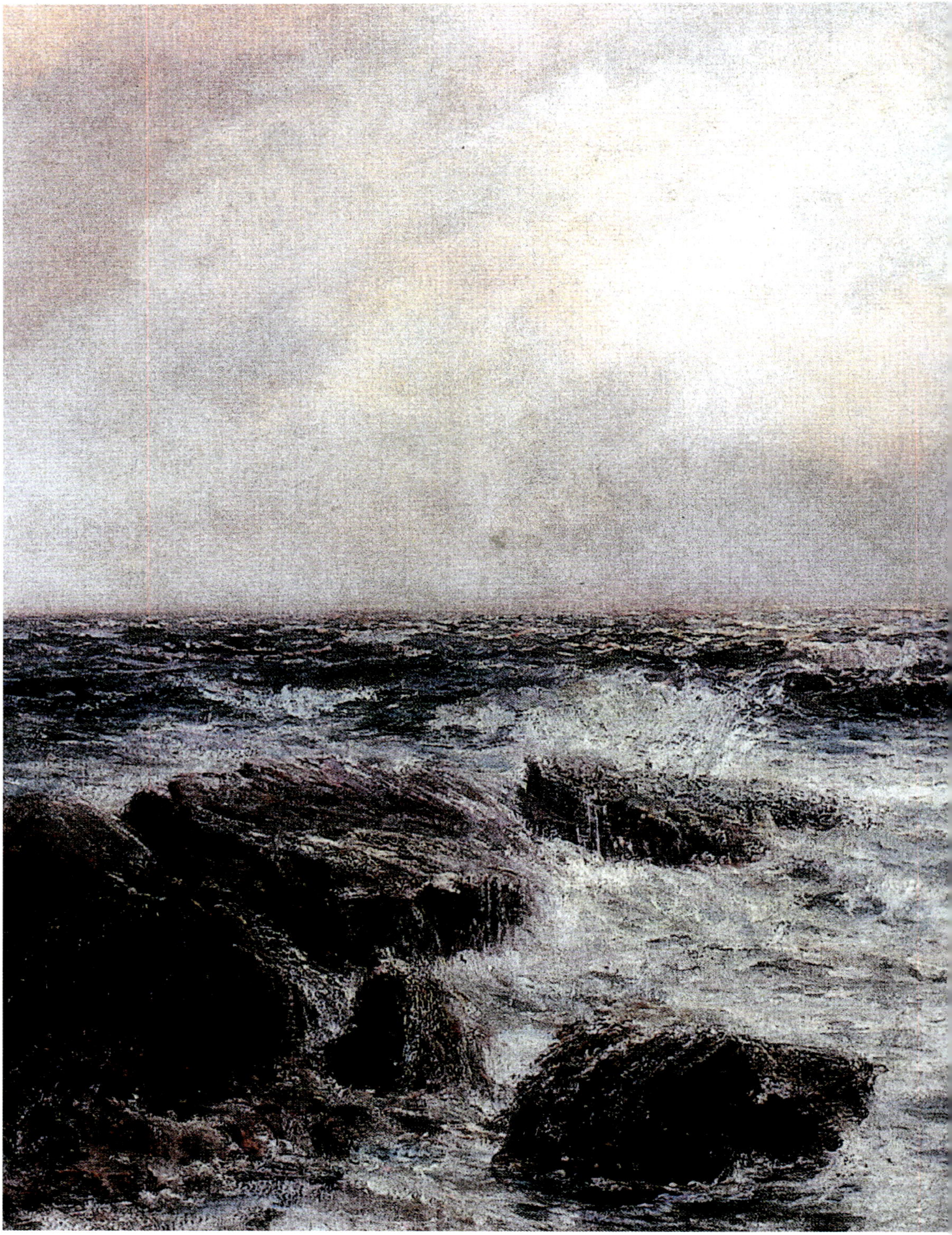

Seascape, 1905, one of Slater's dozens of sea studies painted in the years before his move to the coast.

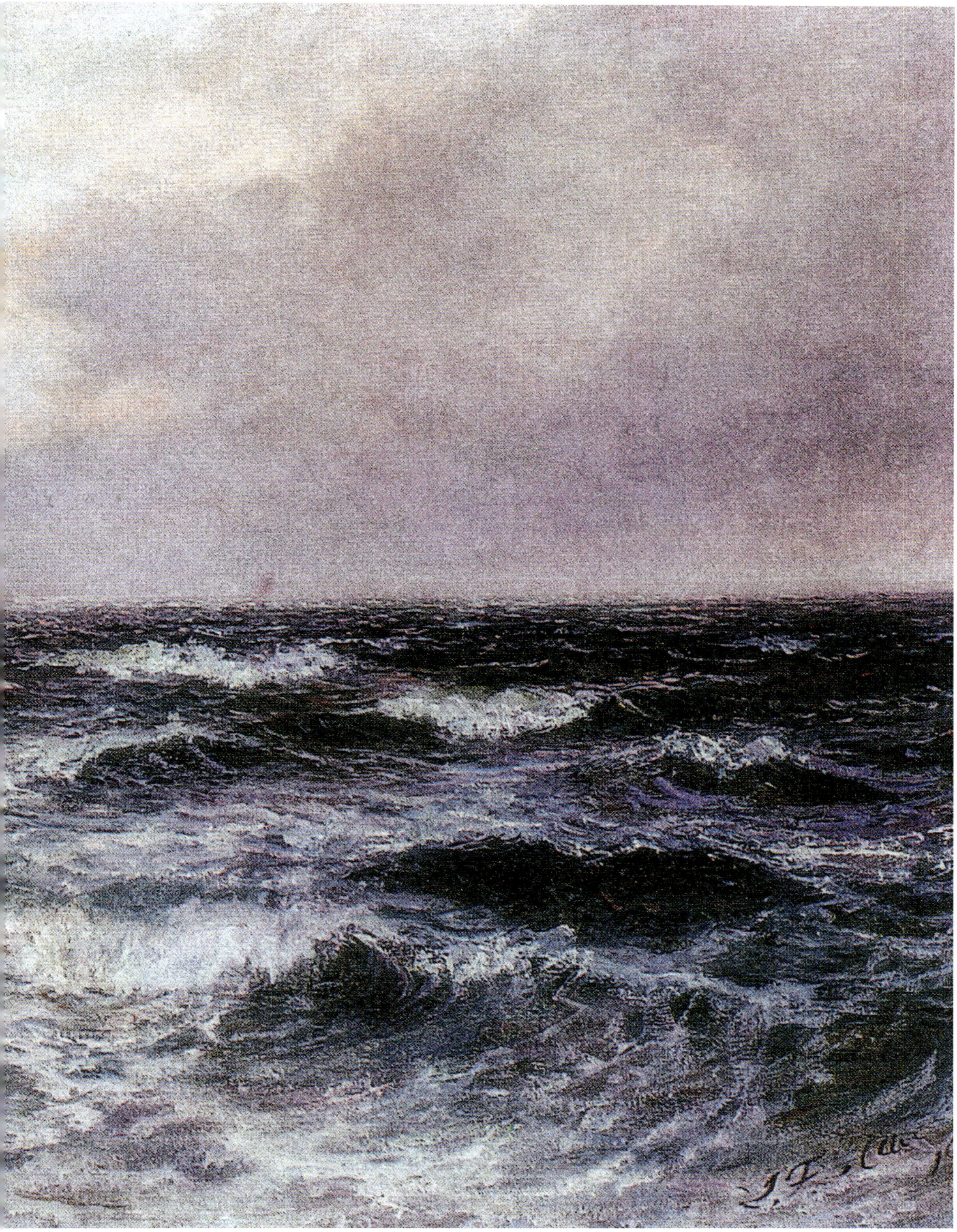

(Tyne & Wear Archives & Museums)

His Move To The Coast

Chapter Six

Following the success of his Cullercoats Bay work, Slater decided to open a temporary studio opposite North Shields Library in Howard Street, and hold a large exhibition of his paintings there[13]. Here he quickly discovered that his work was as popular with local collectors as it was with their Newcastle counterparts, but it was not until 1911, and with several of his local coastal paintings published as popular colour or monochrome prints, that he decided to repeat the experiment of running a studio in this location.

Within weeks of again establishing a studio in Howard Street, he was reinforcing his reputation by sending some of his finest local seascapes for auction at Bainbridge & Sons in the town's Camden Street[14]. This netted him several hundred pounds and provided a nest egg with which to finance moving his family from Killingworth to the coast. By April of that year he had set up home at 6 South Parade, Whitley Bay[15]. However, the property was not large enough to provide a studio, so in 1913[16] he moved home to 15 The Esplanade, in the village, and it was from here that he went out one day in the January of that year to paint one of his most publicised works after moving to the coast.

Its subject was the wreck of the sailing ship *California*, which had run aground 600 yards south of St Mary's Island during a south-easterly gale. Within hours of learning of the disaster, and having first clad himself in his customary ankle-length waterproofs he was standing on the beach with a large canvas perched precariously on his easel. Hardly had he completed his outline of the scene when a small knot of spectators had gathered around to watch him, and such was his celebrity as the 'Weatherproof Artist' that the press photographer sent along to record the wreck returned to his editor with images of Slater (see photo on front cover and page 48) as well as the remains of the *California*[17].

Slater's awareness of the public's interest in himself and his work gave him an idea of how to capitalise on this beyond his paintings and prints. He decided to publish a compendium of his experiences and attitudes as an artist to date. The result was his modest 150-page book entitled *Odds & Ends from an Artist's Note Book*, published by local printers Hewitt & Rudge at their Central Printing Works on North Parade in 1914.

Slater's introduction to the book is worth repeating as an indication of the promptings and intended scope of his book: "A number of my friends have for many years besought me to write a few of my reminiscences. I have, in the following pages, yielded to their importunities,

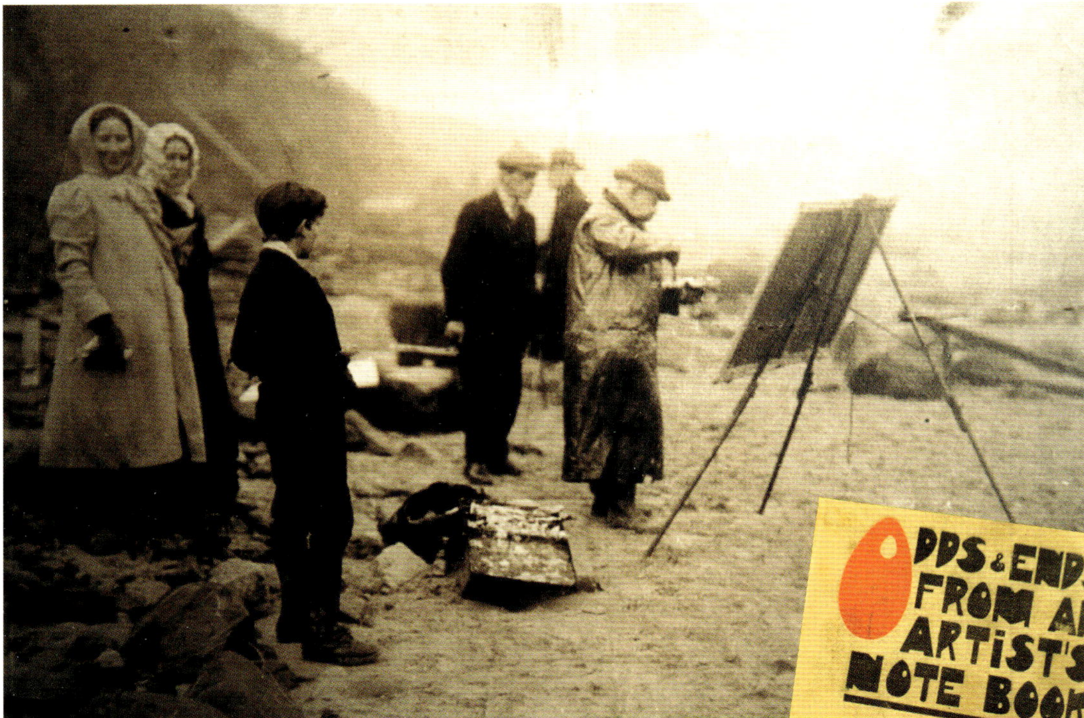

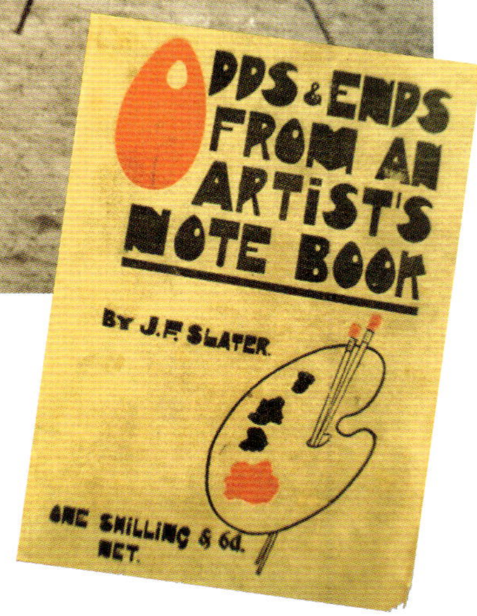

Slater in his typical oilskins while painting the wreck of the California, in 1913. (Dorothy Slater) and, inset, Odds & Ends from an Artist's Note Book, published just before the outbreak of the First World War.

trusting that the Odds and Ends from my note book will not be accepted in any other spirit than that in which they are written, namely, the desire that Art matters may be more generally realised as being important and conducive to intelligent enjoyment, apart from the frequent idea of £.s.d.

"In the various chapters my readers will discover that I have not attempted to describe any methods of painting, but rather the principle which should influence not only the worker but the beholder. I have referred to samples of ideas and opinions, also types of characters about whom, if I have written in a somewhat amusing strain, yet I do not wish it to be thought in an entirely frivolous manner, as I trust the reader will not fail to note the reformation aimed at. I believe contrasts arrest attention, therefore I make use of them to further my object, and trust that my little book may speak for itself to those who may be interested even from curiosity to peruse its pages during some odd half hour."

The book received widespread publicity in the local press and, modestly priced at one shilling and sixpence, it was bought not only by those interested in art, but many who hoped to find in its pages an interesting autobiography of an artist arguably better known to the general public of Tyneside than many others of his period. But in this latter respect they might have

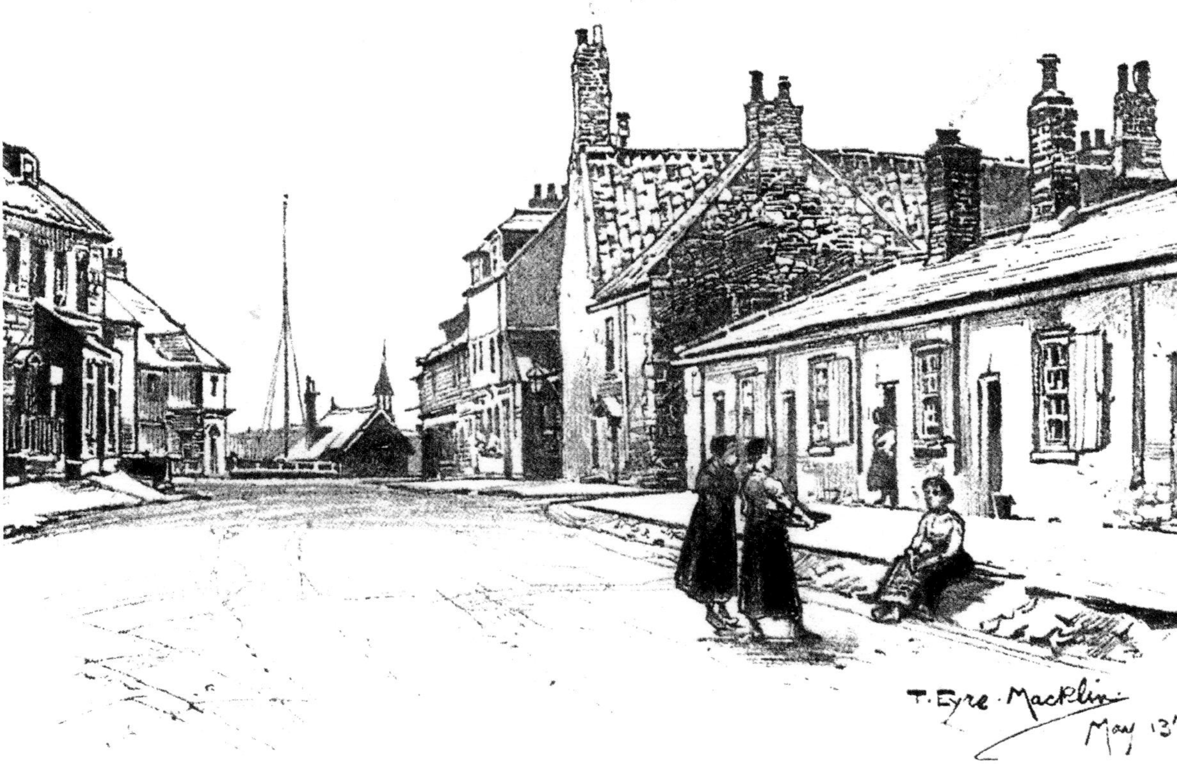

Front Street, Cullercoats, eleven years after Homer had left the village, as drawn by Thomas Eyre Macklin (1863-1943), for Tomlinson's book on the area of 1893. Homer lived at No. 44B, where he rented a single room.

been disappointed. Certainly there are many fascinating anecdotes of his experiences as an artist, but exasperatingly little about his background and subsequent life as a man, as a quick scrutiny of the book's index of contents confirms. Perhaps one of its most interesting chapters, however, is that early in the book headed "Working Experiences".

In this chapter he explains: "For many years I have worked on the coast, more especially in winter, because of the stormy character of the North Sea at that season of the year, which deeply impressed me with the strong emotional charms of cloud and sea, when moved by the nerve-bracing east and south-east winds.

"At first I used small canvasses on which I made my sketches, because of the trying experiences with rain, sleet, and snow. From the sketches I would paint larger pictures, but further knowledge enabled me to work direct on the picture itself on the spot, and so I obtained work which to me was better for possessing spontaneity, vim, and the truth of Nature's atmosphere…"

His penchant for working on large canvasses out of doors had by now become legendary – even allowing for the difficulties of keeping them steady while he painted – and one incident recalled in this chapter was typical of many he experienced over the years: "I have had great

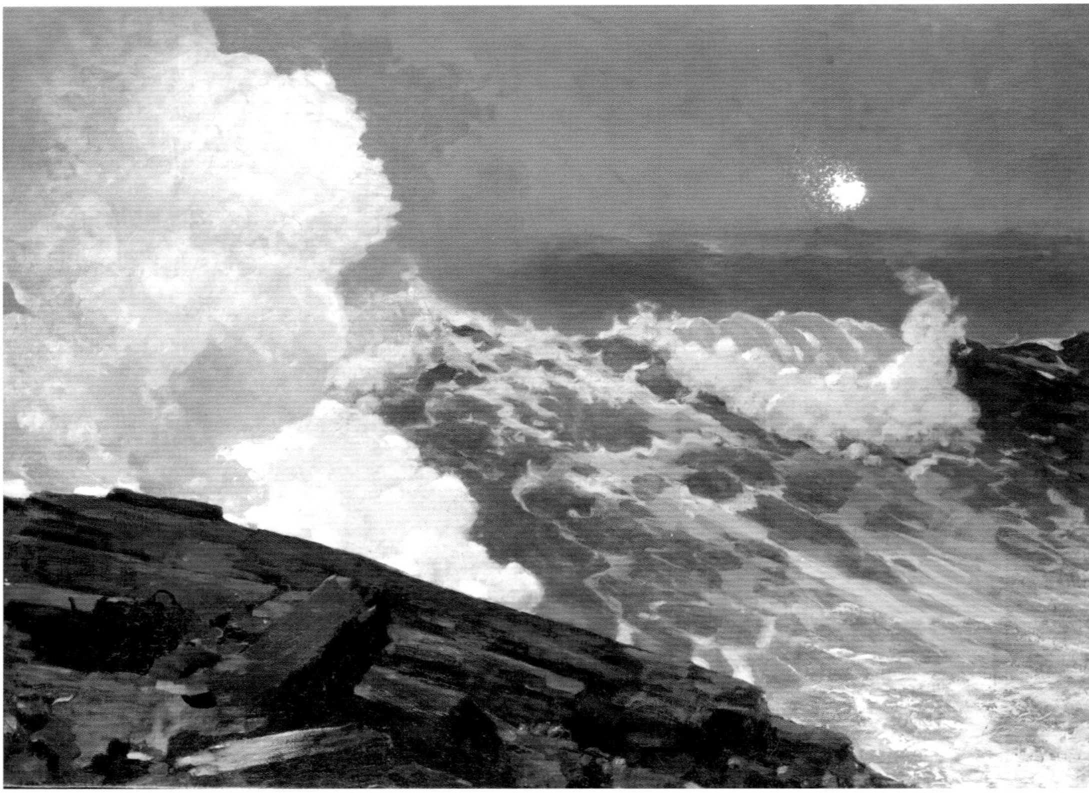

Northeaster, one of Homer's Maine seascapes, of 1895, and, like Slater, showing a complete preoccupation with the sea alone as its subject. (The Metropolitan Museum of Art, USA)

trouble with large canvasses," he wrote. "On one occasion in particular. It was eight feet by five, and I had been out with it in several storms but waited for a rousing gale before finishing it. At last the day arrived, the water was being lashed into fine movement, so I secured the services of a man with a large furniture flat (cart). We tied the canvas firmly on, face up, and with my bag and storm hook easel, set off for the Table Rocks.

"On arrival there, we released our hold of the barrow, when the wind blew it along the promenade. It was with great difficulty that we succeeded in getting the canvas down to the rocks below. We only succeeded by moving it edge to the wind, although we were several times thrown against the rocks.

"My assistant on one occasion thought his arm was broken. However, we finally got it into position by his holding on, whilst I fixed the long ropes around hummocks of rocks, and weighted the canvas with heavy pieces of stone. I told him to look back about 5pm to see if I required anything, when I would have been glad of his help for the wind, increasing in violence, nearly blew my canvas, easel, and moorings away. My assistant eventually arrived, when I told him I thought I could do with him until 6-30, and would then require him to assist me in getting the picture home. I do not remember a harder or more thrilling tussle."

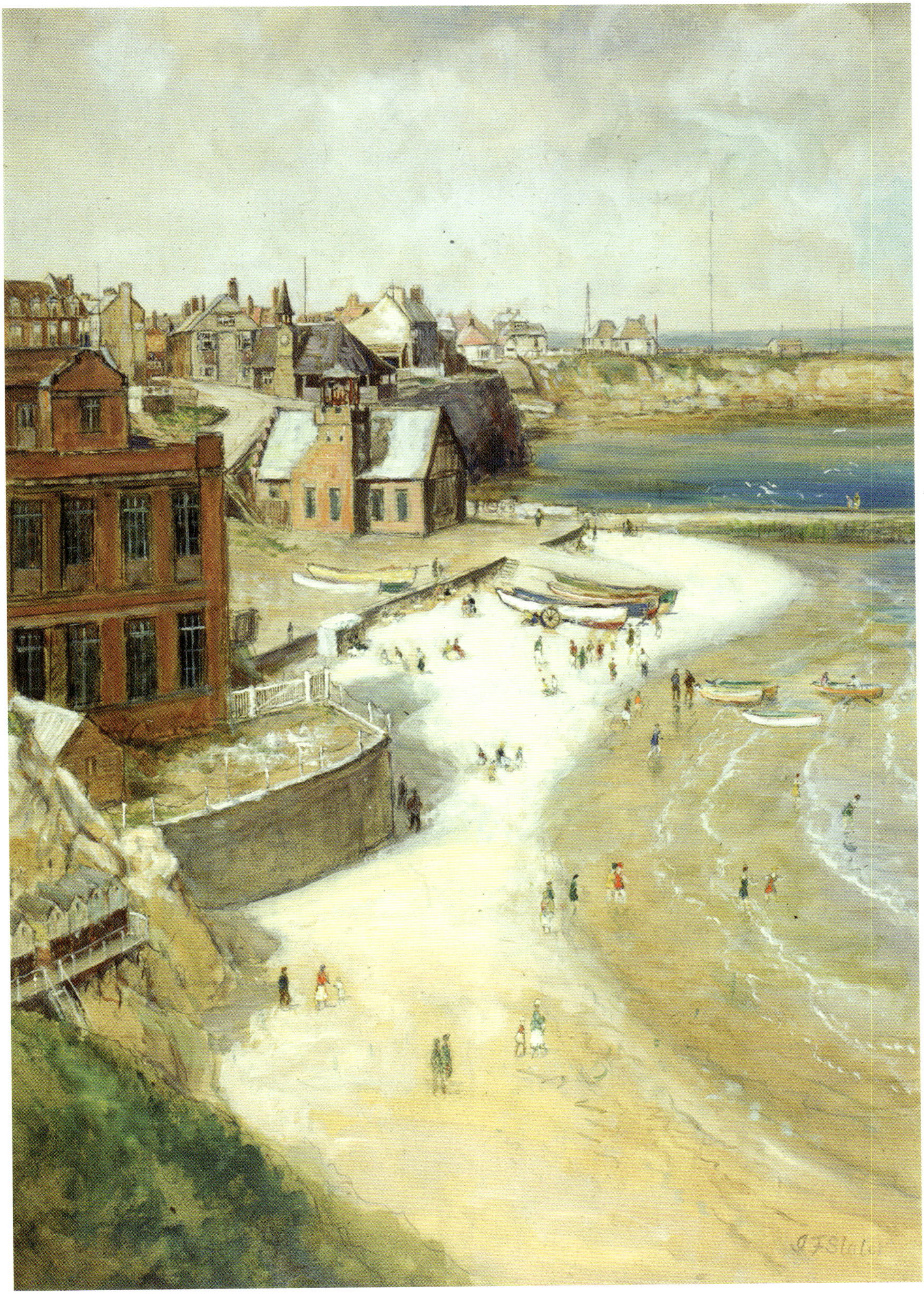

Cullercoats as it looked in 1910. Slater's view of the Bay from the south cliffs. (Tyne & Wear Archives & Museums)

In contrast to the previous page, and other references to his all-weather painting experiences, however, he recounts in the penultimate chapter of the book under 'Pleasant Memories', the following: "An artist friend and I have had many happy experiences when painting about the North East sea coast, also the charming, old-world houses situated on the riverside at North Shields. I recall those pleasant days of work, when, far from the madding crowd, we put in some diligent sketching from the various old gangways in all kinds of weather influenced by the ever-changing scenes of hammering in the docks, the blast of the siren, cries of the free-born sea-birds, and the delightful strains of music borne over the water from voices and band of the well-trained Wellesley boys, all of which, with the rhythmic sound of rowlocks and splash of oars of some passing boat, lent a charm to the hours, richly impressing the mind, speaking of the busy energies of the thews and muscles of the producer, notifying the departure or arrival of some carrier of the busy waterway. The sounds of the commercial world, and softened by the hopeful songs of the young generation being reclaimed and trained to take part in the near future in the workaday, practical world, whilst the frequent calls of the sea-birds in their utterance and wondrously graceful movements, commingles with that harmony of the busy scene.

"Looking back through the quaint old houses to the generations that have passed away from their joys, toils, and sorrows, the imagination is stirred with thoughts of their lives spent hereabouts in those very dwellings, yet amidst conditions greatly different. Then again the remaining few dolphins bring back the tiers of ships moored to them before the days of steam."

The artist friend alluded to as his companion when drawing or painting the old houses of North Shields was, in all likelihood, John Chambers (1852-1928), who shared a similar enthusiasm for them as subject matter for his work. In a later passage in *Odds & Ends* (the frontispiece of which, significantly, is Slater's pencil drawing of the buildings) he alludes to the proximity of this friend's studio to the scene of their endeavours, and Chambers was located at 58 Borough Road, just off North Shields Fish Quay. Further, Chambers was a regular visitor to the Slater home, and sufficiently friendly with the artist and his wife to leave them each a sum of money when he died.

Charles Napier Hemy (1841-1917) shared a similar interest in old riverside buildings, in his case those of the Limehouse reach of the Thames. Inspired, perhaps, by the etchings of James McNeill Whistler (1834-1903), known as the *Thames Set*, Hemy painted or drew his Limehouse river scenes for more than forty years, an outstanding early example being his *London River, the Limehouse barge-builders*, of 1874, in the collection of South Shields Museum & Art Gallery.

But, Hemy was, of course, best known for his sea paintings, indeed, he was by popular consent regarded as the finest exponent of the art in the Britain of his period. So this interest in old

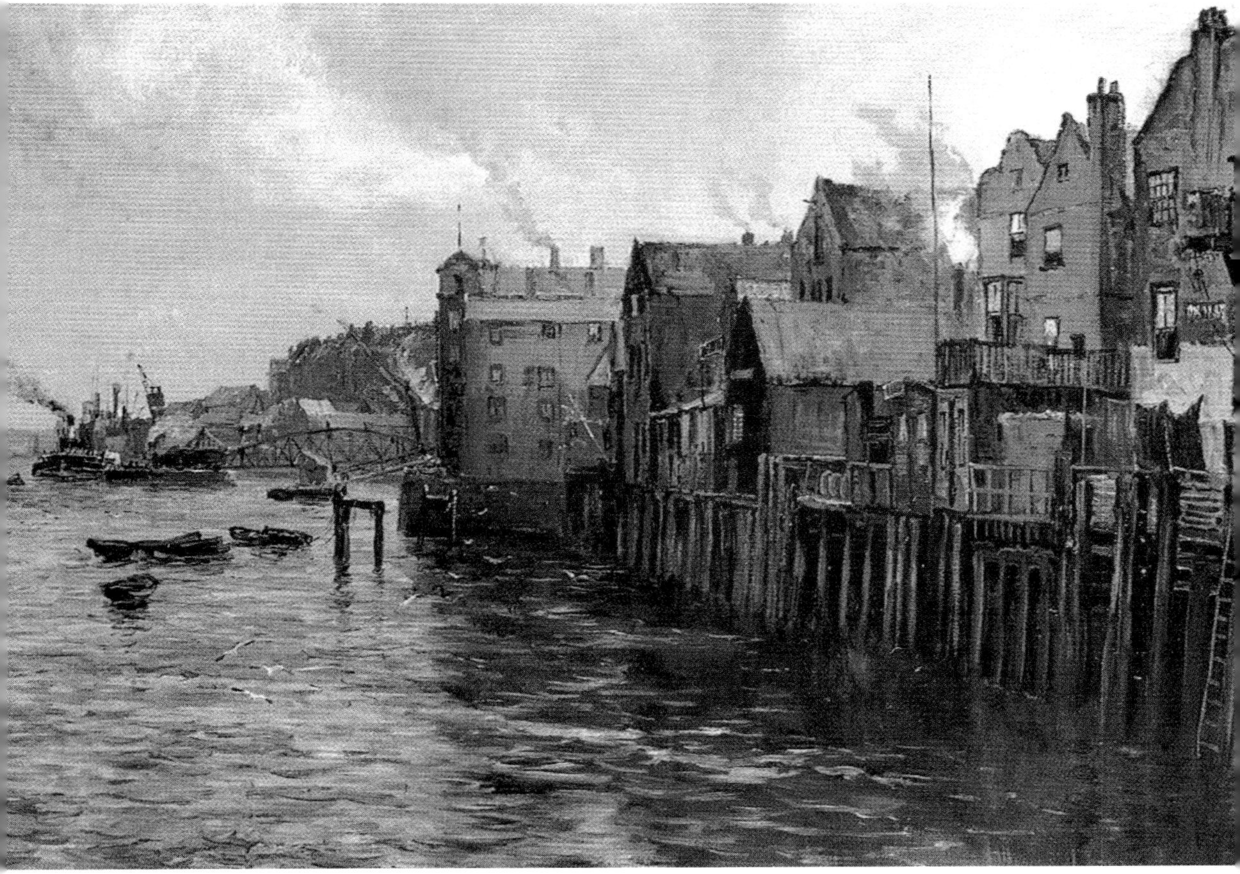

The old waterfront buildings at North Shields in 1911. One of Slater's many studies in oil, pencil, or etching over the years. (Anderson & Garland)

riverside buildings was, like Slater's, a completely contrasting one in terms of the drama of their scenery. Unlike Slater's, however, Hemy's reputation as a sea painter was helped by the inclusion in his work of various sea-going vessels then in use, thereby increasing the interest of potential purchasers of his work.

Slater's reputation, on the other hand, relied almost solely (apart from the occasionally picked out distant sailing yacht) on the appeal of his 'pure' sea pieces. And in this respect his work more closely resembles that of Henry Moore (1831-1895), or Julius Olsson (1864-1942), both of whom were exhibitors with the Bewick Club; Moore in 1884, and Olsson in 1888. Interestingly, however, in referring to the lesser appeal of Slater's sea pieces because of the purity of their content, by contrast the *Whitley Bay Guardian* reported of his 1924 Royal Academy exhibit *The North Sea*, that it was "sold before the actual opening of the exhibition. It is additionally pleasing to know that the picture, a small seascape – typically Slater – commanded a good price."

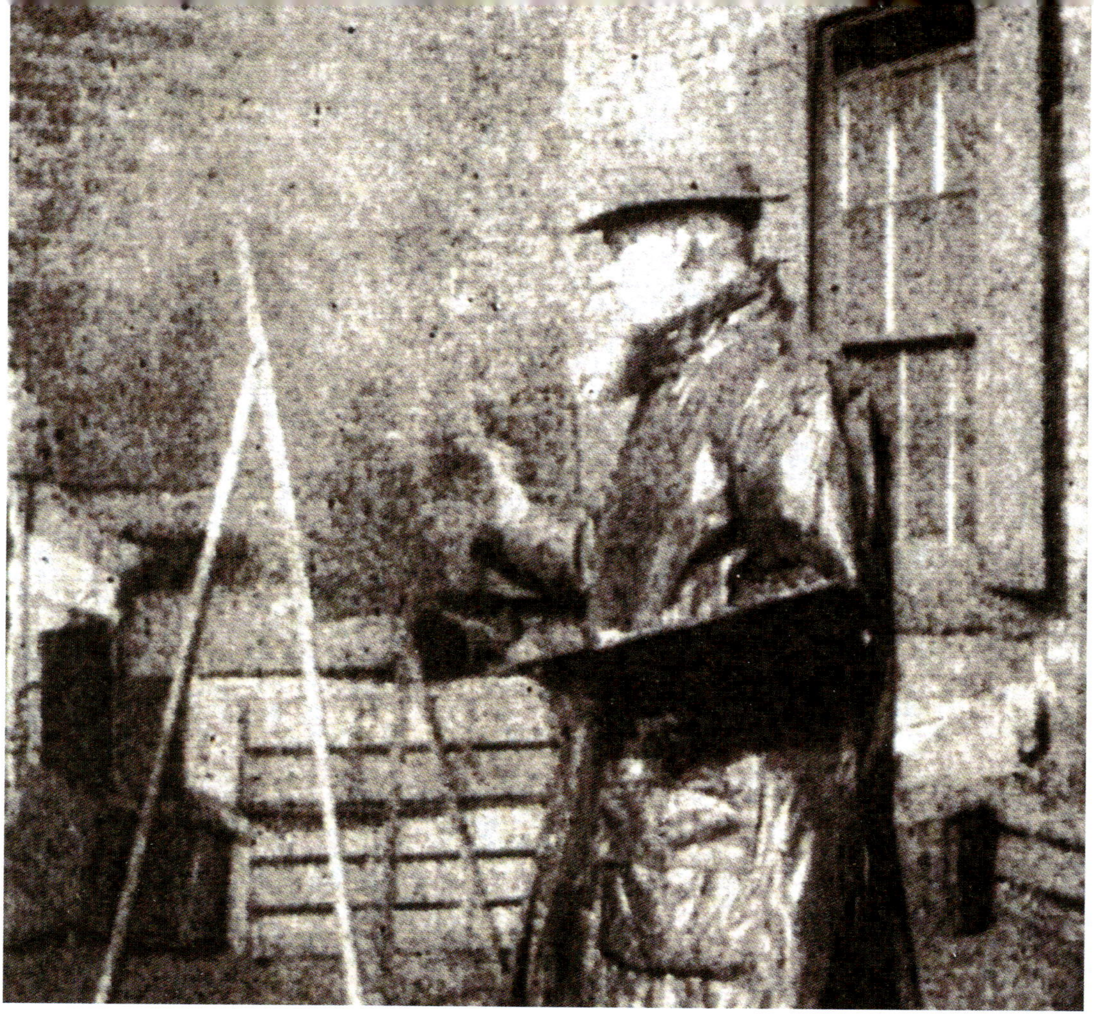

Slater's painting and sketching companion on his visits to the North Shields waterfront – John Chambers (1852-1928), seen here similarly clad to Slater to cope with the frequently inclement weather they encountered. (Keith Bell)

As to the origin of Slater's fascination with the sea - similar to Hemy's, or not - it was the place in which he was prompted to fulfil it, that it is, perhaps, more appropriate to compare with that of his predecessor to the village - Winslow Homer - now regarded as one of America's greatest artists. A great deal has been written of Homer's period in the village - the author, like others, concluding in his article on the subject for *Art & Antiques Weekly*, of December 4th, 1976: *The Quiet American - Winslow Homer in England*, that how and why he chose the village as his temporary home in the country is still not resolved.

Be that as it may, there is little doubt that it was here and in its surrounding coastline that he, like Slater, found his earlist inspiration to paint the sea. Within two years of leaving Cullercoats in 1882 he had settled at Prout's Neck on the rocky coastline of Maine in the USA, only leaving it in winter for visits to the Caribbean to paint. But while most of his seascapes painted at Cullercoats and demonstrated in the Northern Centre for Contemporary Arts exhibition at Sunderland in 1988: *Winslow Homer - All the Cullercoats Pictures*, might be broadly characterised as portraying man's battle with the sea to earn a livelihood from it, like Slater's, his final works painted at Prout's Neck until his death in 1910, concentrated on that much more ancient battle – the battle between sea and land. Said the catalogue of an exhibition of Homer's paintings at the Museum of Fine Arts Boston, USA in 1996: "In them more so than in earlier paintings Homer avoided any suggestion of a story to emphasise the universality of his themes." Slater's, on the other hand, was in evidence from his earliest days as an artist.

When *Odds & Ends* was published he was fifty-seven and, in an era in which that age was considered quite advanced, it could be assumed that Slater wrote it believing that he might not live much longer and the time was ripe to commit a life's experiences to print. However, it must be remembered, counter to this assumption, that two of his children were barely teenagers, and the other two twelve and ten respectively, and would have to be supported for several years to come. His Royal Academy contributions since the turn of the century had continued to confirm his ability as an artist and had all sold well. But although he did not realise it at the time, the outbreak of the First World War in the August of the year in which it was published would have a profound effect not only on the fortunes of the nation, but those of himself and many other artists of the day.

The War Years

Chapter Seven

Recalling the war years many decades later, Slater's daughter Dorothy said: "The Great War was a hard time for us as a family, I and my sister Bertha, and our brothers Thomas and John, were still at school and therefore not yet earning a living.

"Like everyone else in Britain we thought it would all be over in weeks, if not months, so father was not initially worried about his prospects in terms of supporting the family. As time wore on, however, and it became evident that the war was going to last much longer, we often heard mother and father whispering quietly between them about the hard times ahead."

Still living with his family at 15 The Esplanade, Whitley Bay, Slater had continued to exhibit his work in Newcastle at both the Bewick Club, and *The Artists of the Northern Counties* exhibitions at the Laing[18]. His first intimation of the effect the war might have, certainly on the latter's much-valued selling opportunities, came when it was announced that there would not be an *Artists of the Northern Counties* exhibition in 1915. Did this intimate their complete suspension for the duration, as would happen with the Bewick Club's exhibitions?

Laing Curator C. Bernard Stevenson was determined that the exhibitions would be resumed as soon as possible and, although there was again a suspension in 1917, the following year saw their resumption almost uninterruptedly for many years to come. Meanwhile, Slater had the consolation of having no fewer than three works accepted for the Royal Academy exhibition of 1915, and with a significant change in the wording of their titles; each had used the word 'expression' to signify its intentions. Was he rebelling against the increasingly commonplace reference to his work as 'Impressionistic'? Perhaps we should be guided by what he says on the subject in the chapter on "Art Principle" in *Odds & Ends*: "We hear a great deal about impressionism. I am impressed by what I see and what I give out is my expression. I firmly believe in this phase of Art as being the finest in all senses."

Interestingly, this definition of his attitude to painting had earlier been expressed by Van Gogh, who said: "real painters do not paint things as they are… they paint them as they themselves feel them to be," and later by Picasso, who said: "painting is a blind man's profession. He paints not what he sees, but what he feels, what he tells himself about what he has seen."

The 1916 exhibition at the Laing represented another, albeit temporary departure for Slater, this time in terms of his mediums of expression. While again using the word 'expression' in

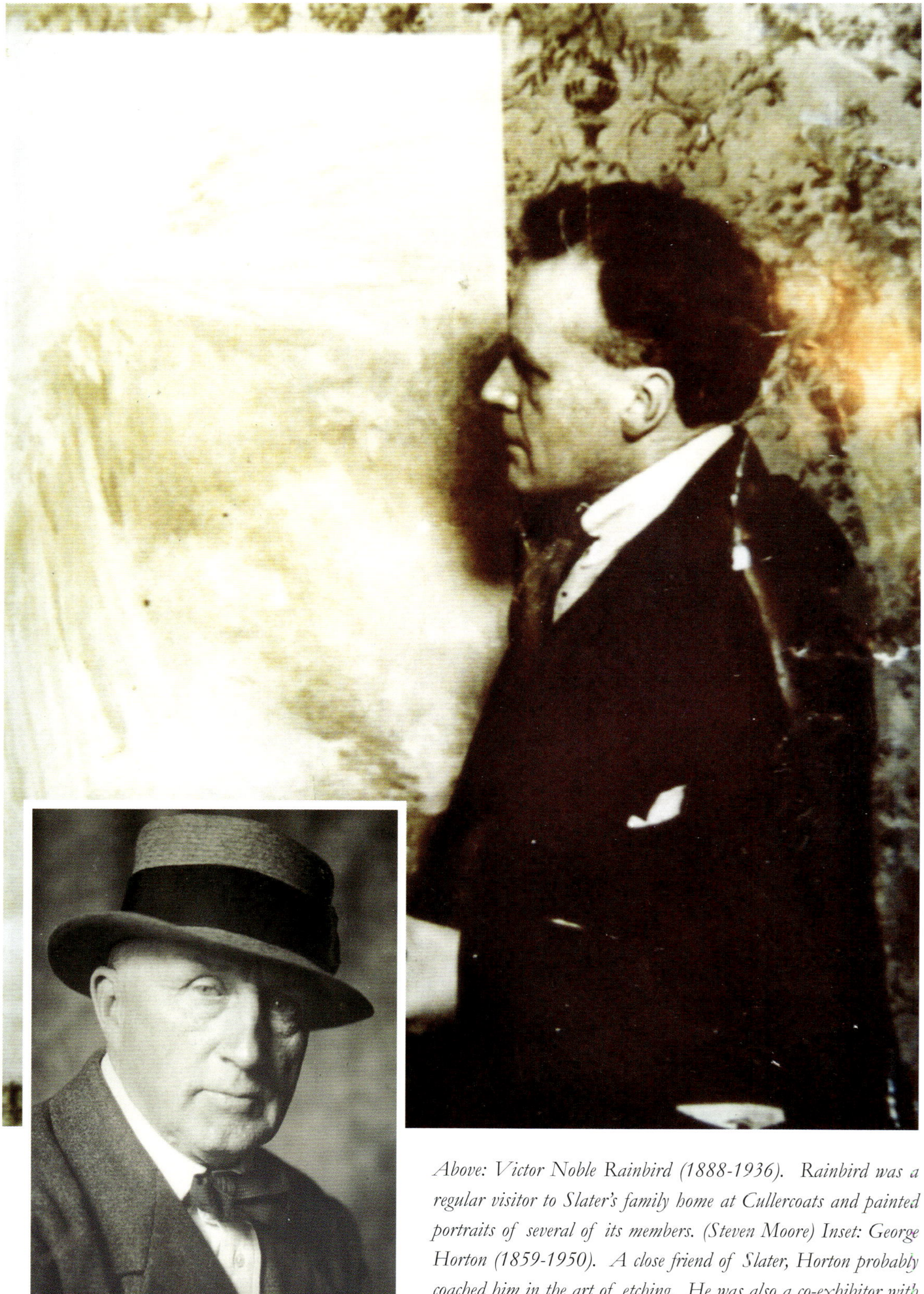

Above: Victor Noble Rainbird (1888-1936). Rainbird was a regular visitor to Slater's family home at Cullercoats and painted portraits of several of its members. (Steven Moore) Inset: George Horton (1859-1950). A close friend of Slater, Horton probably coached him in the art of etching. He was also a co-exhibitor with Slater in the four-man exhibition at the Laing Art Gallery in 1934.

the title of two shown works, one was in tempera, a medium in which he had not exhibited before. A further departure evident in this exhibition, however, was the inclusion of an exhibit, which, like many other artists of the past and present, was designed to offer an example of his work at a more affordable price. For some years now he had been experimenting with the art of etching. Fellow artists like George Horton (1859-1950) – who as a personal friend might well have coached him in the art – had already been successful in selling their work in the medium. Why couldn't he, and particularly in these difficult war-time years when even amongst his usual clientele of professional and trades people money was short?

He sent four of his etchings to the exhibition, but like one of his other experiments of this period, the monotype, it was to prove an only intermittently employed medium of self expression. This involved painting one of his compositions onto a sheet of metal or glass and taking from it an impression on paper. It was a medium which had been employed by several Impressionist artists like Castiglione and Degas, and which he described in a blind-stamped notation on each as part of his 'Expressionist Series'. However, these last were clearly inspired by his constant fascination with experimentation rather than the desire to produce more affordable examples of his work.

As the war drew to a close, and Slater's daughters approached womanhood, the pressing question of their future occupations – if any – arose. They both said they wanted to become schoolteachers and, after each obtaining their teacher training certificates, positions were found for them in local schools. Modest as their initial incomes were, the difference in the family's financial situation would dramatically change. The pressure was off Slater to generate its only source of income from his work as an artist, and having to paint many of the subjects he had been driven to in the past.

Fifty-seven when the First World War broke out, Slater was obviously too old for conscription, but just as he had done in regard to the Boer War he became an avid newspaper reader of its progress. And the first intimation he read that it would not be over as quickly as he, and many others thought, was a statement by then British Foreign Secretary Edward Grey: "The lamps are going out all over Europe. We shall not see them lit again in our lifetime." Thankfully, old as he now was, this was not to be true of Slater's lifetime; he survived for almost 20 years after its conclusion in 1918.

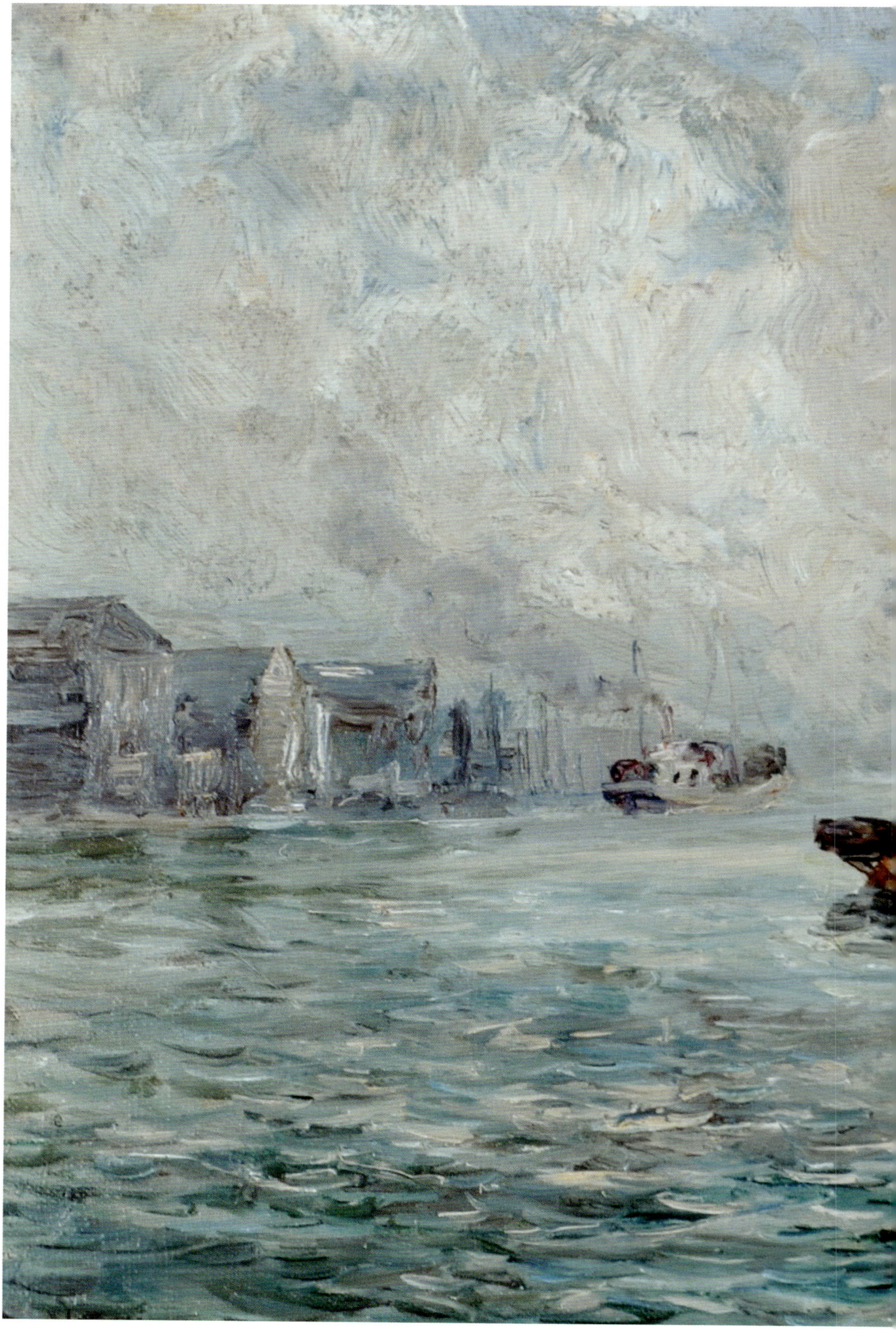

The Tyne Tug 'Wonder' at North Shields, one of the many paintings of tugs and other vessels at the mouth of the Tyne Slater executed over the years, as well as general views of the entrance to the river. (Anderson & Garland)

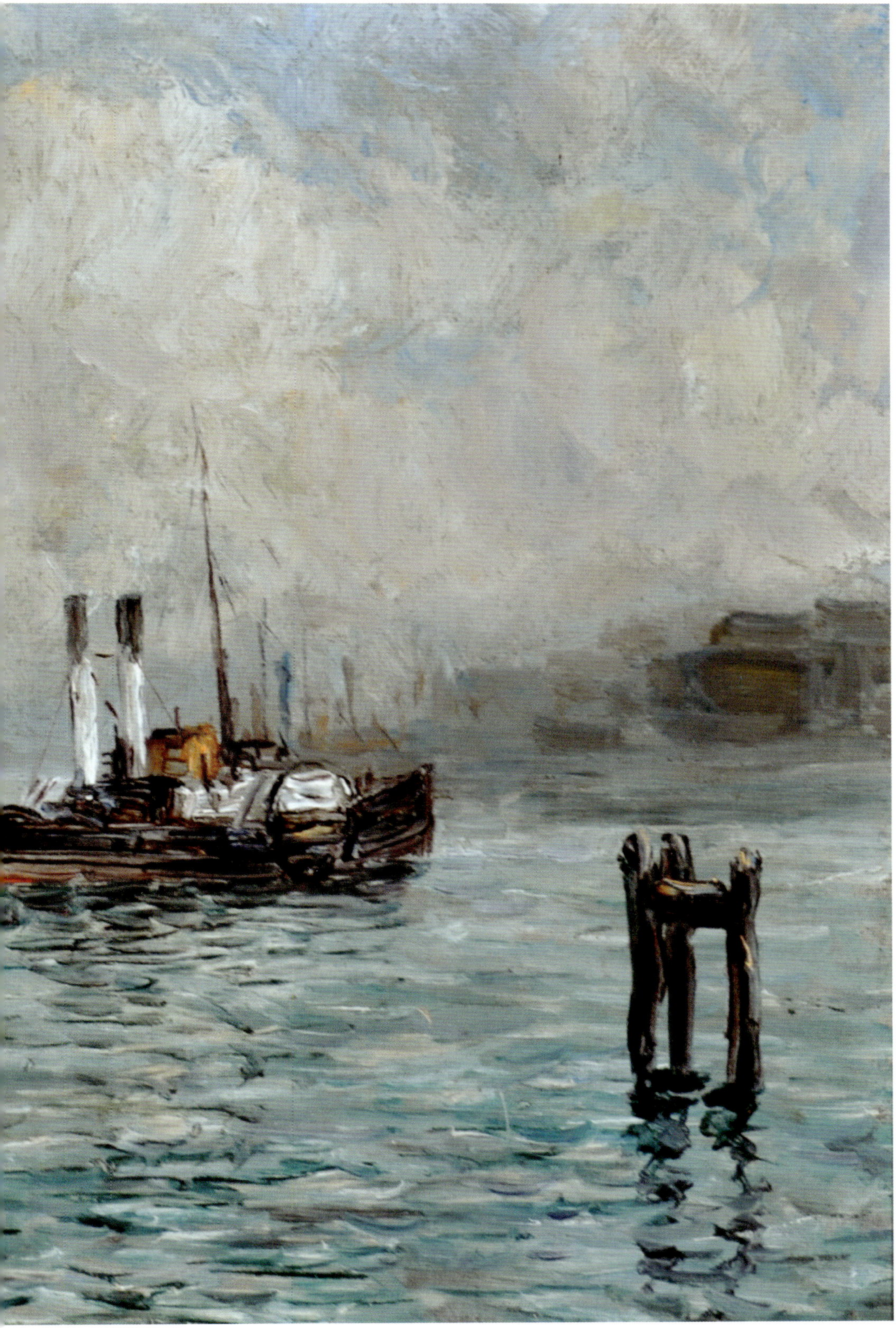

A Decade Of Achievement

Chapter Eight

Aged 63 as the decade of the twenties got underway, Slater still had surprises for his admirers. The first thing he did was to found a new art club for the area - The North East Coast Art Club. An ambitious project which some doubted would survive much longer than its earlier local counterparts (Tynemouth Art Club, founded in 1883, which was a development from the Tynemouth Fine Art Association of 1879, and South Shields Art Club, founded in 1891, both of which had long effectively expired), the Club founded by Slater would flourish for some forty-three years.

Disappointingly, its first exhibition in 1920, and, indeed, several subsequently, did not strike critics as doing very much more than provide a showcase for amateur work. Said the *Shields Hustler* in its issue of autumn 1926 "it is encouraging to see the work of local amateurs at the Exhibition held annually at the Old Council Chambers at Whitley Bay… (but) the work of many local artists of note were conspicuous by their absence." Slater, of course, as founder and president of the club showed his work at its every exhibition. But reassuringly four years later in the same publication this same correspondent was reporting "of recent years the exhibition has attracted considerable crowds of art lovers, and some very fine works have been displayed."

That Slater welcomed the exhibiting interest of amateurs is of little doubt. He was able to offer them classes at which he could help them improve their technique for only a small sum per class – and this was useful additional income. But it also generated another idea for increasing his income – designing a small, collapsible easel that he could sell to his students for their outdoor sketching.

After months during which he produced several prototypes, a final version was ready, and an ingeniously designed piece of equipment it turned out to be. Collapsing to a size which would easily tuck under the arm or be slung over the shoulder, it not only incorporated an easily adjusted easel, but a comfortable padded seat. He dubbed it the 'ABC easel', but although its metal label included in its description the words 'PATENT APP. FOR', the Patents Office has been unable to confirm that it was ever granted patented status. Some fifty or so were produced by a local joiner, and while most found ready buyers, he was left with at least four examples which remained with the family until they were auctioned in recent years.

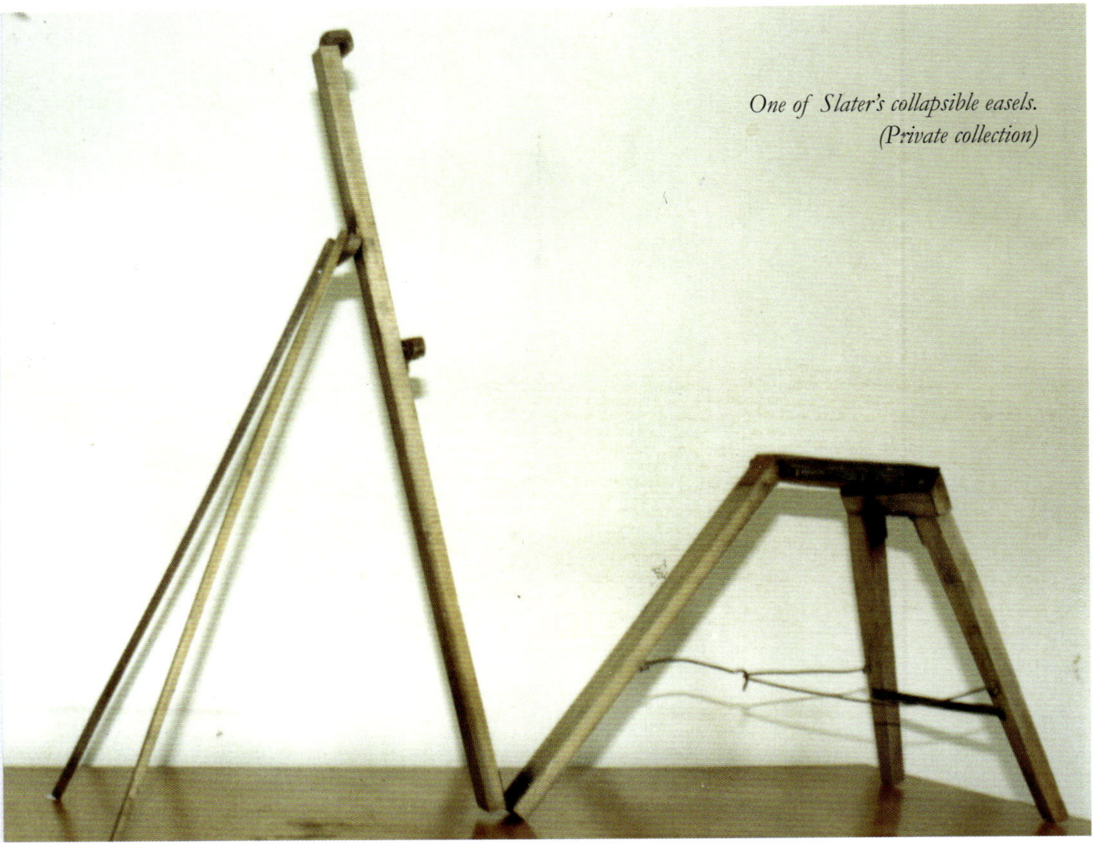

One of Slater's collapsible easels. (Private collection)

As the decade progressed, Slater found himself in increasing demand as a portrait painter, and whilst a number of his sitters were Tyneside worthies whose likenesses were commissioned by local institutions, two examples not in this category generated more than the usual publicity. The first was of no less a person than the inventor of the modern equivalent of the telegraph machine – Frederick George Creed (1871-1957); the second, local hero Robert ('Scraper') Smith (1849-1927), coxswain of the motor lifeboat at North Shields.

Said a local newspaper in 1923 of the Creed portrait: "Mr John F. Slayter (sic), the well-known North Country artist, has just added a fine portrait to the many previous successes he has achieved in this branch of the art. It is that of Mr F. G. Creed, of Croydon, the inventor among other things of the type tape machine which bears his name and which is in use in most up-to date newspaper offices.

"The portrait which is to be on exhibition for a short while at the premises of Messrs Browne and Browne, art dealers, Grey Street, Newcastle, is a striking likeness as those who know Mr Creed certify. But it is something more than a mere likeness. It has a vitality and character, as indeed, most of Mr Slayter's portraits have, since they are invariably direct paintings of the subject and not paintings from photographic studies.

"Mr Slayter's command over his medium is demonstrated by the fact that he executed the portrait of Mr Creed in less than three hours, but as Whistler would say, to put into that small

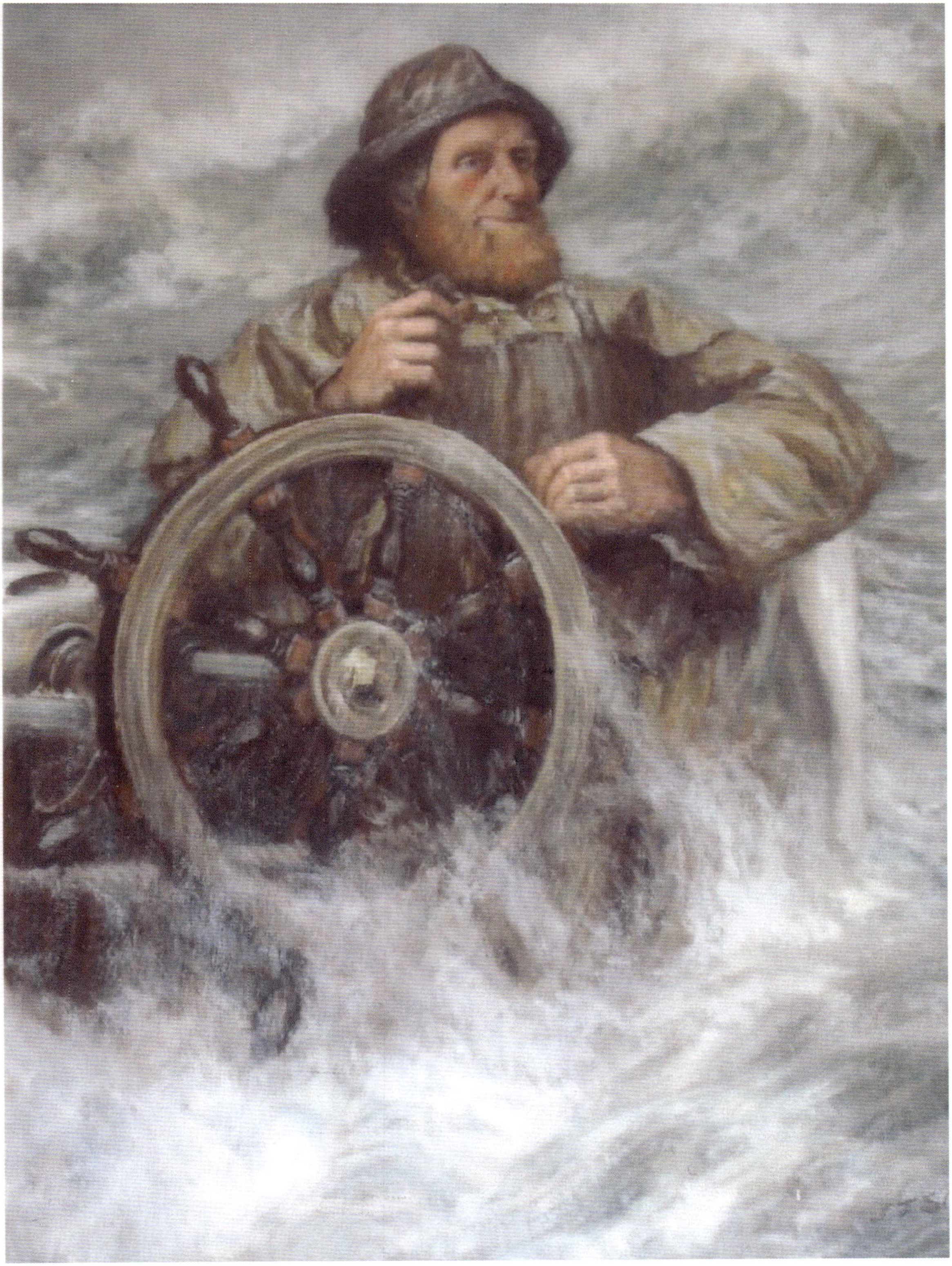

"Scraper Smith", one of Slater's best-known portraits of the 1920s. (RNLI)

compass many years of experience. The study relies on its appeal solely as a portrait, having no trappings to give exposure for brilliant colours and contrasts[19]."

The portrait of Smith was treated to a similarly flattering description in the *Shields Daily News* following its execution a year later, accompanied by an illustration of the legendary coxswain's portrait. "The picture is a reproduction of an oil painting by Mr J. F. Slater, the artist, of Mr Robert Smith of Cullercoats, formerly coxswain of the motor lifeboat at North Shields, who was honoured by the King on Monday. The painting is exhibited in the art shop of Messrs Browne and Browne, Grey Street, Newcastle. It will perhaps rank as one of the most successful of Mr Slater's productions, the portraiture is clever, for the individuality of the old lifeboat man stands out with lifelike effect on the canvas. Moreover, the setting is perfectly ideal. The tempestuous sea which Mr Slater delights to portray is here the background for human energy and courage embodied in the typical east coast figure of Coxswain Smith.

"It is to be hoped some effort will be made to have the picture displayed at the seaside. In any case, it is gratifying that so wonderful a record has been executed by so accomplished an artist, of one who is reckoned among the heroes of the north east coast." Smith's claim to fame was, of course, his role in saving 50 lives from the hospital ship *Rohilla* in 1914 in a terrible gale off Whitby. This feat won him the Empire Gallantry Medal[20].

Gratifying as these flattering comments about his portraits must have been they were, perhaps, eclipsed in terms of the pleasure they delivered by a piece which appeared in the prestigious arts magazine *Drawing & Design* the year before the first of these was painted. Appearing in its October 1922 issue, and accompanied by a photograph of a beach scene which he had just painted, it said: "Mr Kenneth Glover, M.S.A., sends us the above picture as an example of the work of another Northern artist who, like George Horton, is comparatively unknown outside the North. Mr Glover ventured the opinion that Whistler or Manet would not have been ashamed to acknowledge the authorship of such work which is certainly remarkable[21]."

The beach scene in question was one of several small-scale studies of day visitors to the beaches of Tynemouth, Whitley Bay and Cullercoats, which Slater produced in the early 1920s and are outstanding for two reasons. The first is that, together with those produced by a few other local artists, notably John Atkinson (1863-1924) and George Horton (1859-1950), they did not focus on the fishing activities and people of the area as had those of earlier artists, and secondly, they were in a style resembling that of several other contemporary artists now commonly recognised as outstanding British Impressionists – notably Philip Wilson Steer (1860-1942).

Much of Slater's work to date could readily be deemed 'Impressionist', but these were quintessentially so, and he later painted several much larger works following Monet's death in 1926, and which might in today's parlance be described as 'tribute' paintings. One was even

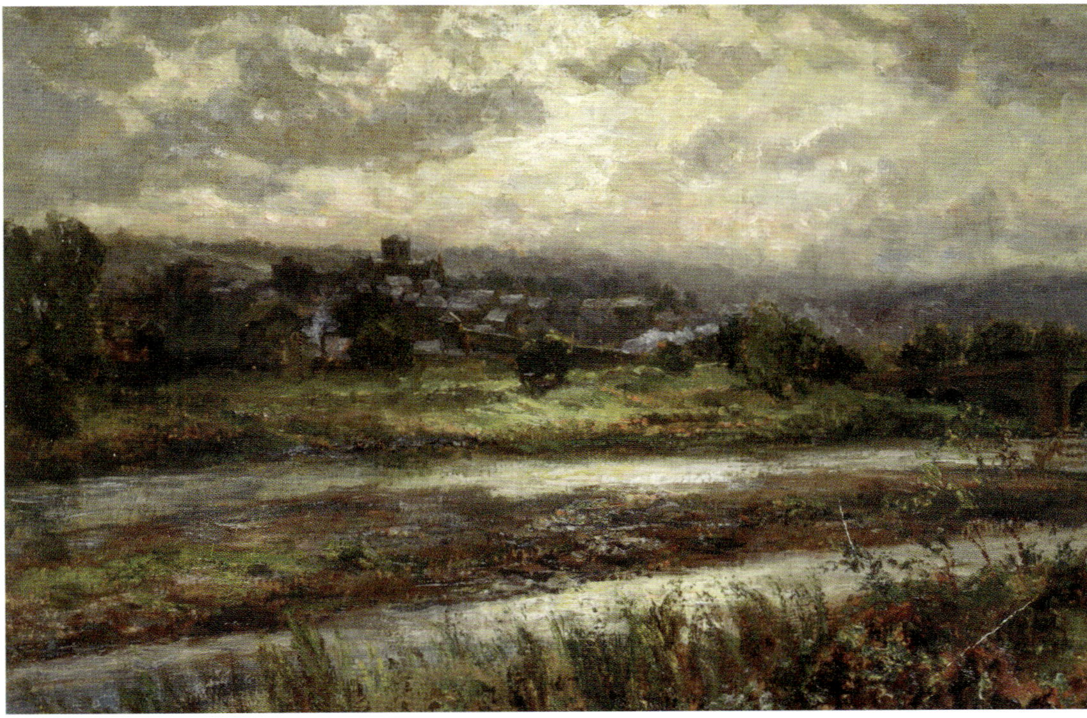

Slater's Hexham - shown at the North East Coast Exhibition and later donated to the Laing's permanent collection.
(Tyne & Wear Archives & Museums)

titled *A Back Road to Giverny*. These paintings gave rise to the widespread, but according to his daughter Dorothy, inaccurate impression that he had earlier visited Monet's home area and painted them on the spot! But just to confuse his followers he had another and contrasting work to put before them – his first known Biblical scene, and one painted in a purely traditional manner.

Said the *Shields Hustler* in January 1928: "Our old friend Mr J. F. Slater, whose versatility as an artist knows no bounds, is at present engaged on an allegorical picture which teems with interest." The piece then goes on to refer to the place in which the correspondent had seen it in progress, 19 St Oswin's Avenue, Cullercoats, Slater's new home of some two years and the location of his studio.

"He has gone to the Bible for inspiration in the case of his allegorical work, and his picture-sermon is based on two texts, the first being the 8th and 9th verses of the 21st chapter of Numbers, which give an account of the rebellion of the children of Israel who were punished by the plague of fiery serpents. When they confessed, Moses was ordered to make a serpent of brass and hang it on a pole, and when any bitten person looked upon it he, or she, lived. The other text is to be found in the 14th and 15th verses of the 3rd chapter of St John, where the Lord states as Moses lifted up the serpent in the wilderness, even so must the Son of Man be lifted up that whosoever believeth in Him should not perish but have everlasting life.

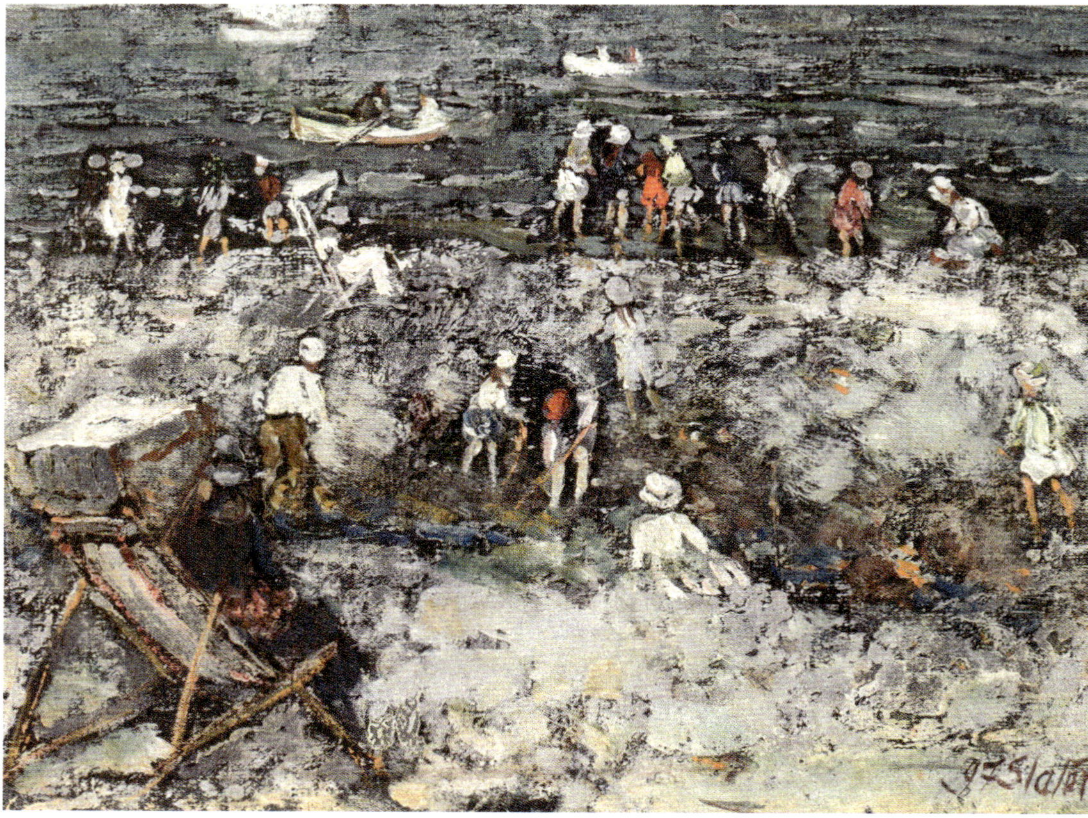

The beach scene of 1922 illustrated in Drawing & Design. (Private collection)

"In the foreground of the picture are the stricken people in various postures, whilst a young man striding over to them points with rapture to the serpent bidding them to look and live. In the radiance of a rainbow Calvary is to be seen in the distant sky. The whole picture sparkles with colour, and life, and although not quite finished is well worth seeing and studying. Mr Slater will gladly show it to you if you call at his studio. He is anxious to have expressions of opinion on not only from the artistic standpoint but from the religious."

The house in which Slater's visitor had seen the unfinished painting was the modest, mid-terrace property into which the family had moved from their previous home in Lish Avenue, Whitley Bay, and which Slater's daughters had bought for them in 1924. It was only minutes from the sea at Cullercoats, indeed one of its upstairs rear windows framed the sea almost like a Slater painting. But just as important as its location in one of Slater's favourite painting places – Cullercoats – was, as Dorothy Slater would recall to the author with pride decades later, it was the first home the family actually owned.

The years of the decade saw Slater's career as an artist reach its peak. Now in his early seventies he would see his name and particulars regarding his career and life included among some 4,450 such profiles of living British artists published in a dictionary; show his work at a prestigious North East exhibition to more people collectively than had seen it to date at every other exhibition in which he'd participated, and have one example from that occasion accepted for the permanent collection of the Laing Art Gallery.

'Mr Dolman's directory', as *A Dictionary of Contemporary British Artists*, 1929, edited by Bernard Dolman, was quickly dubbed, immediately won praise from the art press. Said *The Connoisseur*: "For some time the want of a directory dealing exclusively with artists and critics, experts, curators, collectors and dealers, has been apparent, though the formidable task of preparing such a volume has doubtless deterred publishers from embarking on the subject. This omission, however, has now been adequately filled…Tastefully mounted (the directory) has leapt at a bound into the position, from which it will not be easily dislodged, of a standard work of reference essential to any well equipped art library."

Described on its title page as 'a series of Alphabetically Arranged Biographies of the leading Men and Women in the World of Art', Dolman, then editor of the *Art Trade Journal*, had completed a mammoth task. It proved so popular that the publishers (Dolman's employers) were encouraged to publish a second edition within two years.

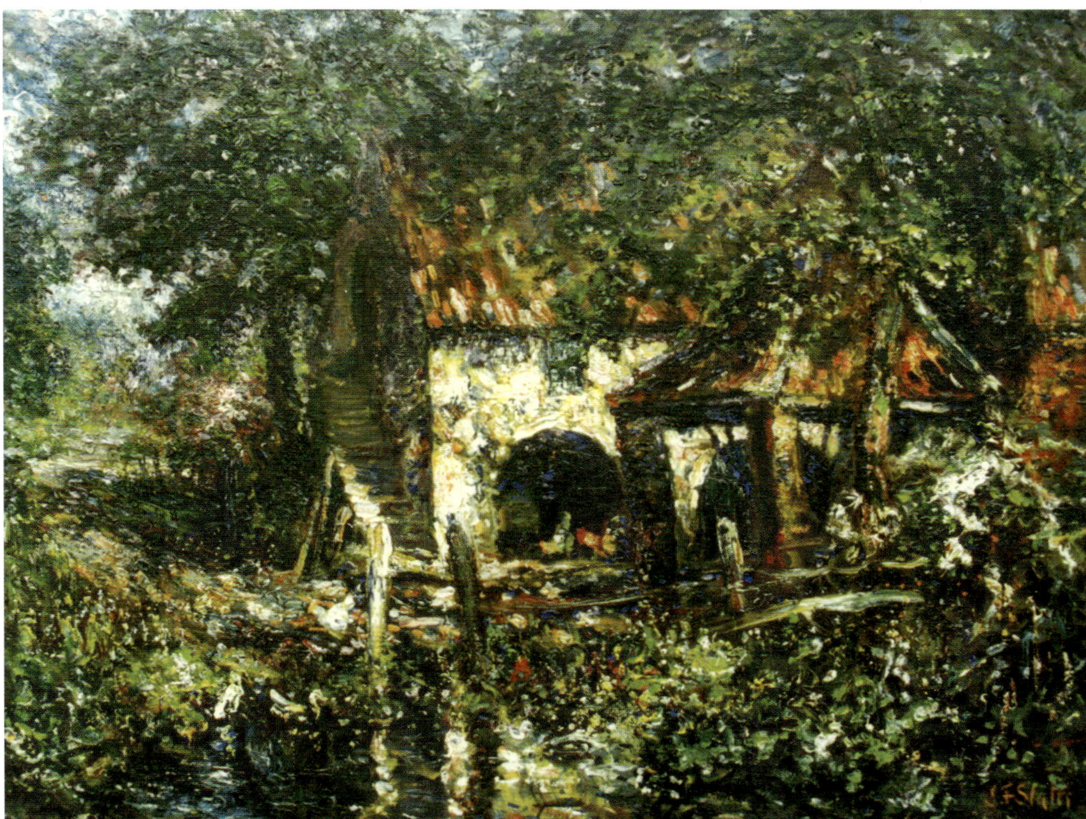

A typical Monet 'tribute' picture painted in the late 1920s. (Private collection)

Like every other living artist included in the book Slater had been identified for his importance by being sent an entry form which enabled Dolman to formulate his wordings. The entries included comprise a veritable Who's Who of British Artists of the period, and Slater, who eagerly bought a copy, found his name and particulars sandwiched between those of other artists who are today household names[22].

The North East Coast Exhibition, held from May to October 1929, in Newcastle's so-called Exhibition Park, included three of Slater's works, of which one in particular won him widespread attention, and its eventual donation to the Laing Art Gallery by its purchaser. His pictures were shown alongside those of his contemporaries, both local and national, in what was described as 'The Palace of Arts'. Located on the north side of the ornamental lake of 1887, (which had been incorporated in the exhibition layout), it had to be enlarged due to the massive response to the appeal for loans of works of art mounted by its organisers.

The large central hall of the building and its radiating galleries displayed paintings, etchings and sculptures, photographs and silverware. Works by numerous famous British and Continental artists of the past and present were loaned by local art galleries and private collectors, such as the Duke of Northumberland, those by names such as Lely, Reynolds, Canaletto, and Millais hanging alongside works by dozens of living local artists like Slater, who had seized the opportunity to show at this prestigious venue, opened along with the rest of the exhibition by H.R.H. The Prince of Wales, on Tuesday 14th May 1929[23].

More than 4 million people would attend the exhibition by its close on Saturday 26th October, and over 500,000 of these would see and hopefully admire in the Palace of Arts the massive oil of Hexham which Slater showed alongside two of his more modestly proportioned works: *Jesmond Dene*, and *An Expression of Morning.*

It was a work measuring 8 feet (244cms) wide and completed (as he would describe in his talk to Newcastle's Pen & Palette Club on 2nd March 1935) "between the hours of 1.30pm and 6pm", on the spot[24]. Like another of his other two contributions however, the oil was definitely not for sale. It had been unofficially loaned by one of the earliest local collectors of his work – Newcastle businessman Angus Watson – who would recall in his autobiography *My Life*, published in 1937:

"I still have the first picture that I bought, a painting by J. F. Slater, and I am not ashamed to have chosen it forty-five years ago. It was called 'Rothbury Moors', and portrays a carrier's cart drawn by two horses crossing the fells from Alnwick. I was pleased to buy a beautiful example of his work much later entitled 'The River at Hexham' and this I presented to the Laing Art Gallery, Newcastle." Angus (later Sir Angus) Watson, like many other Newcastle collectors of the period, was no mean judge of works of art. By the time he wrote his

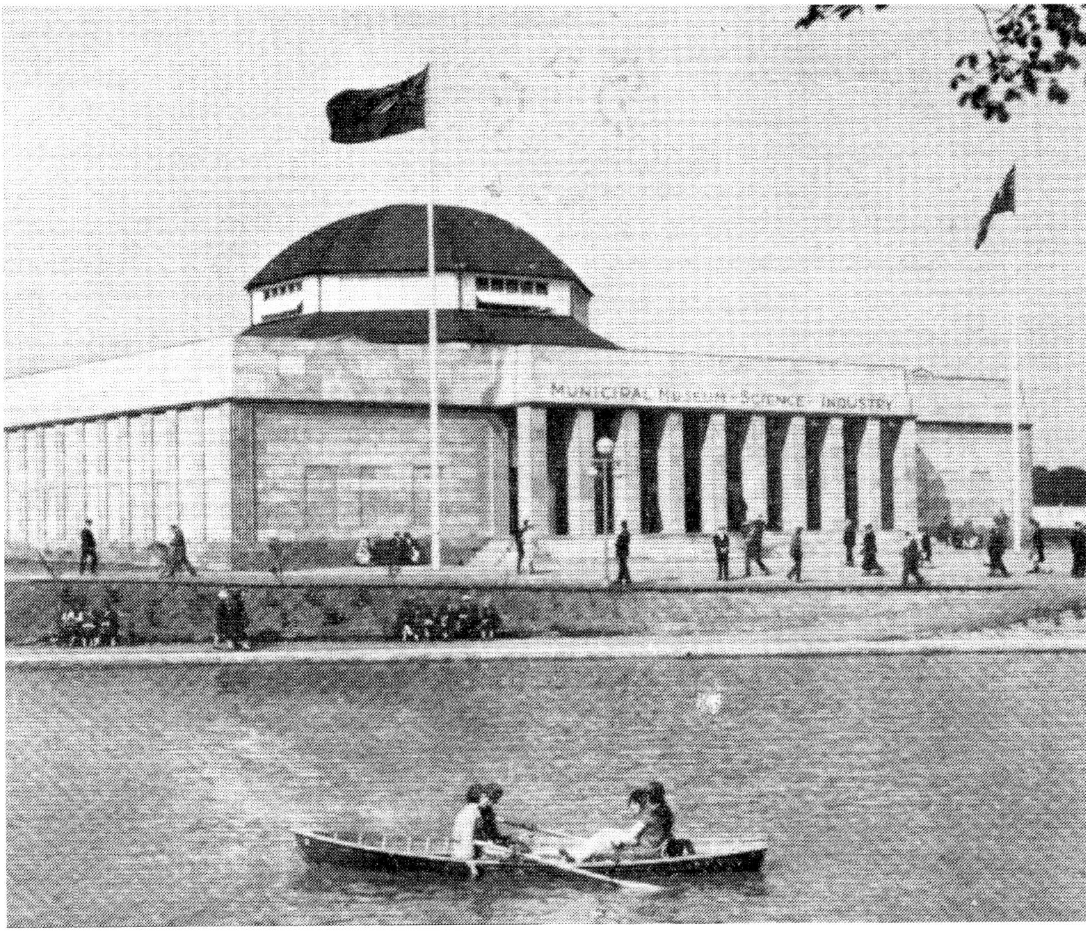

The Palace of Arts at the North East Coast Exhibition of 1929. It is today the only surviving building from the event.

autobiography he was 63 and whilst still working in his Newcastle office could comfortably afford to indulge his tastes in collecting everything from medals to paintings, thanks to a considerable fortune he had amassed through his company's sales of 'Skippers Sardines', and other food products from its Tyneside base[25].

"I possess a lovely example of Lucy Kemp-Welch's work 'Farming in Winter', which I first saw at the Royal Academy," he would write in his book, "and I have a good example of Isobel Coddington's robust painting that is generally considered to be one of her finest pictures.

"I have also a delightful painting by Dame Laura Knight from which I get continued pleasure, and two beautiful pictures by Harold Knight, her husband, both of which were hung in the Academy." A perceptive collector indeed.

The Final Years

Chapter Nine

Although Slater's final years of life would begin quite auspiciously with the donation of his Hexham oil to the Laing Art Gallery's collection in 1930, the economic outlook of the region, in common with the nation generally, was far from reassuring. The 1929 North East Coast Exhibition had certainly helped to some extent redress the economic decline of the area – shipbuilding, in particular, being an immediate beneficiary, but what of the years to come?

What has since been dubbed the Great Depression had already started, and the nation was still holding its breath as to whether the Labour minority government led by Ramsay MacDonald, and elected in the month the exhibition closed, could do anything to deal with the situation. Meanwhile as the 11th exhibition of the Art Club he had founded at Whitley Bay in 1920, opened its doors to the public in the autumn of 1930, with Augustus John RA as Honorary President and himself as President, Slater must have been too distracted to dwell on much more than its hoped for success.

Had the balance between the number of amateurs which its organisers had earlier been accused of allowing access to exhibiting, and those local professional artists whom its accusers thought should be represented, been adequately addressed? The answer must surely have been yes, for among those showing their work in this first exhibition of the new decade were well-known local professionals including Thomas Bowman Garvie (1859-1944), John William Gilroy (1868-1944), James Doxford (1899-1978), Victor Noble Rainbird (1888-1936), Dixon Clark (1849-1944), and Eva Carter (1885-1963).

The venue of the exhibition had also changed in character, being no longer the Old Council Chambers, but Imperial Buildings, on South Parade, Whitley Bay, where also it continued to hold the club's "Lectures, Demonstrations and Life Classes during the Winter Months". Subscriptions were still ten shillings and sixpence per year, and members were entitled to the "use of studios at any times during the day". In the same year, however, another longstanding series of exhibitions was temporarily suspended by one of the vice presidents of the club – C. Bernard Stevenson; the *Artists of the Northern Counties* exhibition at the Laing, of which he was, of course, curator, did not take place in 1930, but was held over until the following year. However, another Newcastle art exhibition of 1930 may have been a consolation to local gallery goers.

Wrote Joseph Wallace Black (1884-1945), amateur artist and publisher of this and many other pieces about Slater in his periodical free sheet the *Shields Hustler*, in its Autumn issue 1930:

"I am under a debt of gratitude to my friend J. F. Slater for taking me to Armstrong College at Newcastle to see an exhibition of modern art. The exhibition consisted of a small private collection of British and French pictures in oils, all of which had a distinctive individuality.

"I cannot write of Art as an outstanding authority, but I have a keen appreciation of beauty in any form, and some of these pictures are singularly beautiful. If you ask me What is Modern Art? I would be somewhat at a loss to put the answer into words. I feel what it is in my being, but giving expression to what I feel is quite another matter."

Contradicting his modesty in claiming his lack of authority in writing of art, Black went on to single out several works – notably those of Walter Sickert, Augustus John, and Matthew Smith – for comments that were both perceptive (and unlike those of several other visitors, remarkably in advance of current popular taste). However, of perhaps greater interest is his final paragraph, in which he said, obviously prompted by his visit to the exhibition: "I have seen two of Mr J. F. Slater's portraits in modern style, and my friend seems to be imbued with the spirit of youth and modernity, although he has passed the allotted span. He has caught the spirit of the new movement in his pictures, and the tonality of these two portraits impresses one with its complete harmony. Mr Slater has never been in a groove, and is determined to keep pace with the modern movement in art, and I would advise you to ask him to show you these arresting portraits."

Slater's visit to the Armstrong College exhibition was one of only dozens of trips he had paid to his native city since moving to the coast, either to see his work on show at the Bewick Club, or the Laing, or much more often simply to socialise. And he must have been a striking figure in his early years of this practice notwithstanding his modest height of only 5ft 6ins. Two of his favourite destinations on his social visits were the café run by relatives of the family, Slater and Potts, close by St Nicholas's Cathedral, and Tilley's Restaurant on Blackett Street. Indeed, so fond of the latter did he become as a social destination that he even painted a picture of its interior together with fellow diners! Of course occasional calls at the Laing to see Stevenson were mandatory, both to discuss North East Coast Art Club Committee affairs, and possibly pave the way to future purchases; and across the road from the gallery's entrance on Higham Place, there was always a warm welcome to be had from members of the Pen & Palette Club.

Slater had even more pressing reasons to see the Laing's curator in the early weeks of 1934, however. Discussions had begun regarding a four-man exhibition later in the year involving himself, Thomas Bowman Garvie (1859-1944), George Horton (1859-1950), and Frank T Carter (1853-1934) – all long-standing friends, and all of an age deserving some recognition for their individual artistic achievements. It was to be a loan exhibition, and while a number of potential lenders had already heard of the proposal and been in contact with Slater, many had yet to be identified to the Laing so that letters inviting their loans could be written.

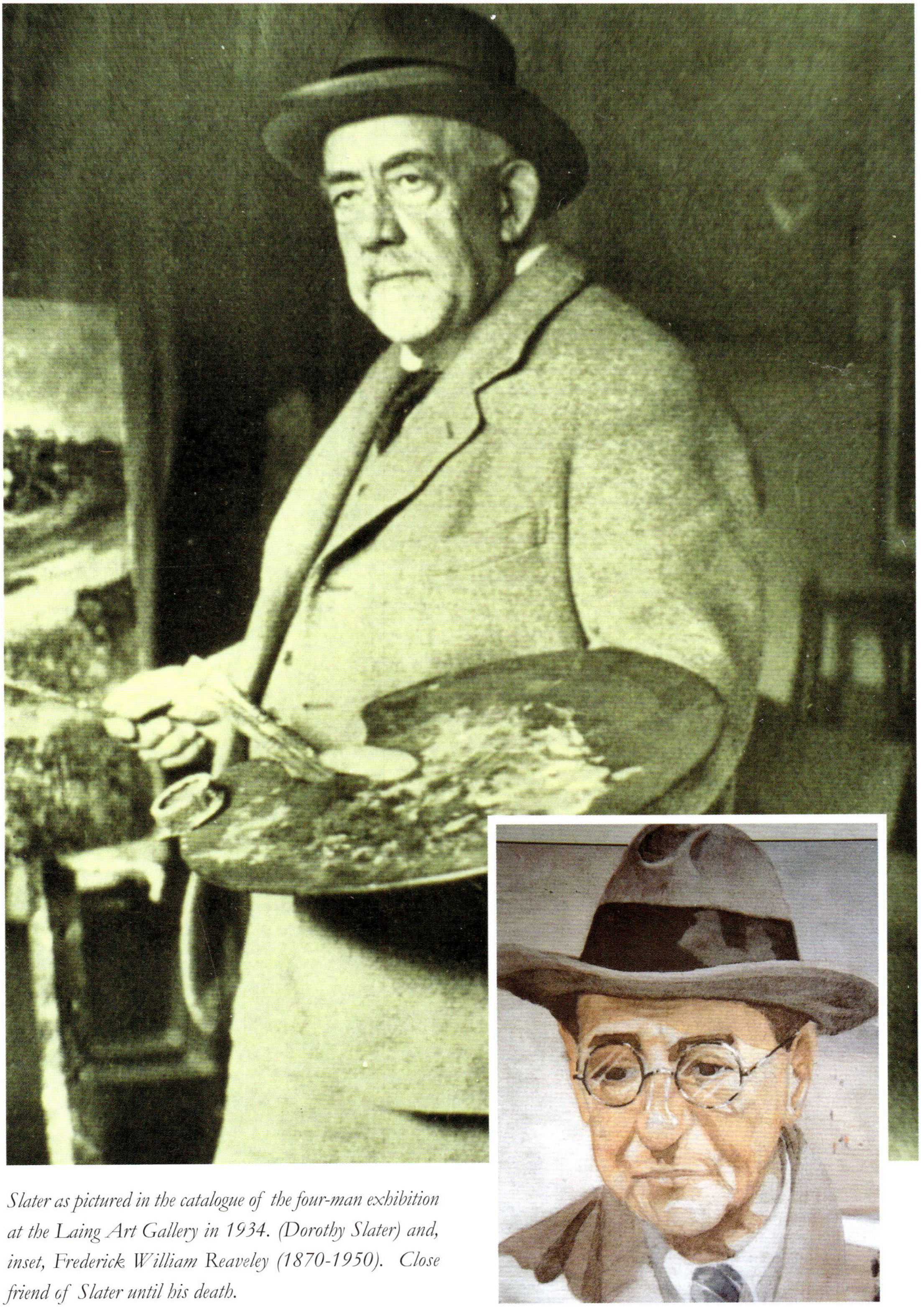

Slater as pictured in the catalogue of the four-man exhibition at the Laing Art Gallery in 1934. (Dorothy Slater) and, inset, Frederick William Reaveley (1870-1950). Close friend of Slater until his death.

Nothing could have better demonstrated the wide range of collectors of Slater's work than the resulting exhibition. It revealed to the general public, perhaps for the first time, not only his outstanding ability as a painter, but the varied patronage his work had enjoyed in his lifetime. Local gentry, businessmen and industrialists, eminent physicians and well-known art collectors allowed their treasures to appear on his behalf.

Some 98 works in oil and tempera by Slater were on show in the exhibition, reflecting not only this diversity of ownership, but the many less characteristic paintings which advancing age and the difficulties of working out of doors in all weathers had prompted him to produce in recent years. Flower, garden, farmyard and portrait studies were much in evidence alongside his earlier sea pieces. "As I moved about the gallery," wrote one local journalist of the exhibition "I felt a pride in John F. Slater and North Country art. His wife and family were there to do him honour and he freely talked to numerous admirers. He seemed to radiate happiness in the event, surely one of the supreme moments of his long life."[2]

Perhaps out of an awareness of Slater's advanced age at which the exhibition had taken place, and the few years which might be left to him, he became increasingly approached for press interviews or comment. Several of these interviews appeared in newspapers published locally and one which appeared in the year following the exhibition, and to coincide with his 78th birthday, was typical of these.

Said the *Seaside Chronicle*, March 1st, 1935: "What an interesting man Mr Slater is – so a friend, after having his first chat with him exclaimed to me.

"Slater, (everybody knows him as that) can talk, as well as paint, in fact he has frequently lectured and is a charming conversationalist.

"'Whatever you are going to say about me please be modest,' he pleaded, and Mr Slater still lives modestly at St Oswin's Avenue, Cullercoats, close to the sea he loved so well and which he has painted in all its varying moods.

"He is now 78 years old and has 28 (sic) pictures exhibited at the Royal Academy London…

"He has been a familiar figure on the rocks and sands, catching the sea in its phases. Even the most stormy mood, Slater has been there with his 'storm easel' and tackle – very necessary in severe weather. In this way Slater gave way to his wonderful gift and when given the inspiration works intensely and with extreme virility. Virility is in his nature – you notice this when he discusses a subject…

"Mr Slater is a gentleman who lives for his art – and his art lives with him. His undoubted talent has characterised the man, who has served a real purpose in life which has been truly worthwhile. He has made the world richer by his conception of the grandeur of the sea, the

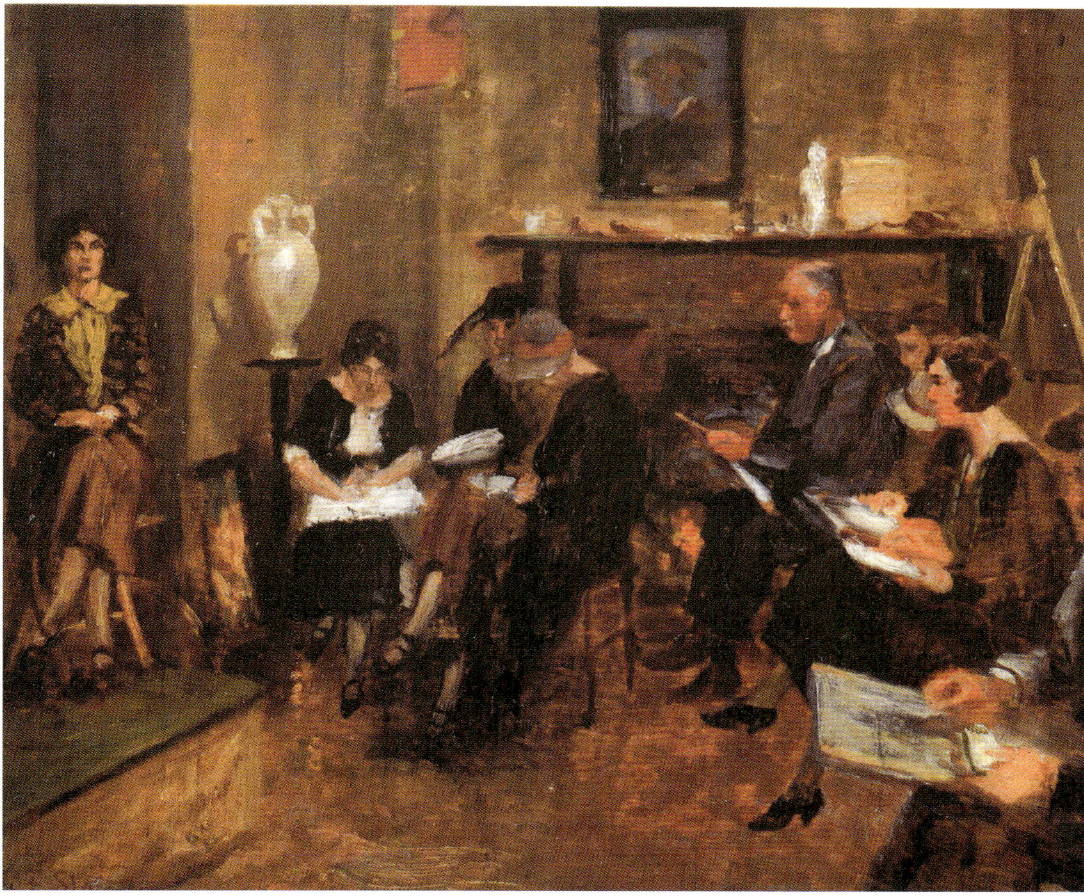

Members of the North East Coast Art Club as painted by Slater at one of his teaching sessions. (Bob Batey)

rugged glen, and the richness of the bloom of flowers."

Despite his growing infirmity, Slater remained faithful to the aims and activities of the North East Coast Art Club to the last, rarely missing meetings and showing work at its exhibitions until just before his death. And he must have been particularly gratified in the year after the Laing exhibition to read in the *Evening Chronicle* on September 6th, not only of the general high quality of the club's exhibits, but reference to the inclusion of the Biblical study he had painted back in 1928, and which had since hung in his home in Cullercoats.

Said the paper of this (yet untraced) rare excursion into religious painting – rare considering that for years he is said to have "preached to the Brotherhood", in and around Newcastle: "The veteran president of the Society, Mr J. F. Slater, is well represented, and his Biblical picture in oils 'The Life Message….' is bound to attract reverential attention…"

With increasing ill-health, and his last intended Royal Academy exhibit behind him (his *River Tyne* of 1936), Slater might now have considered whether his exhibiting career, indeed his

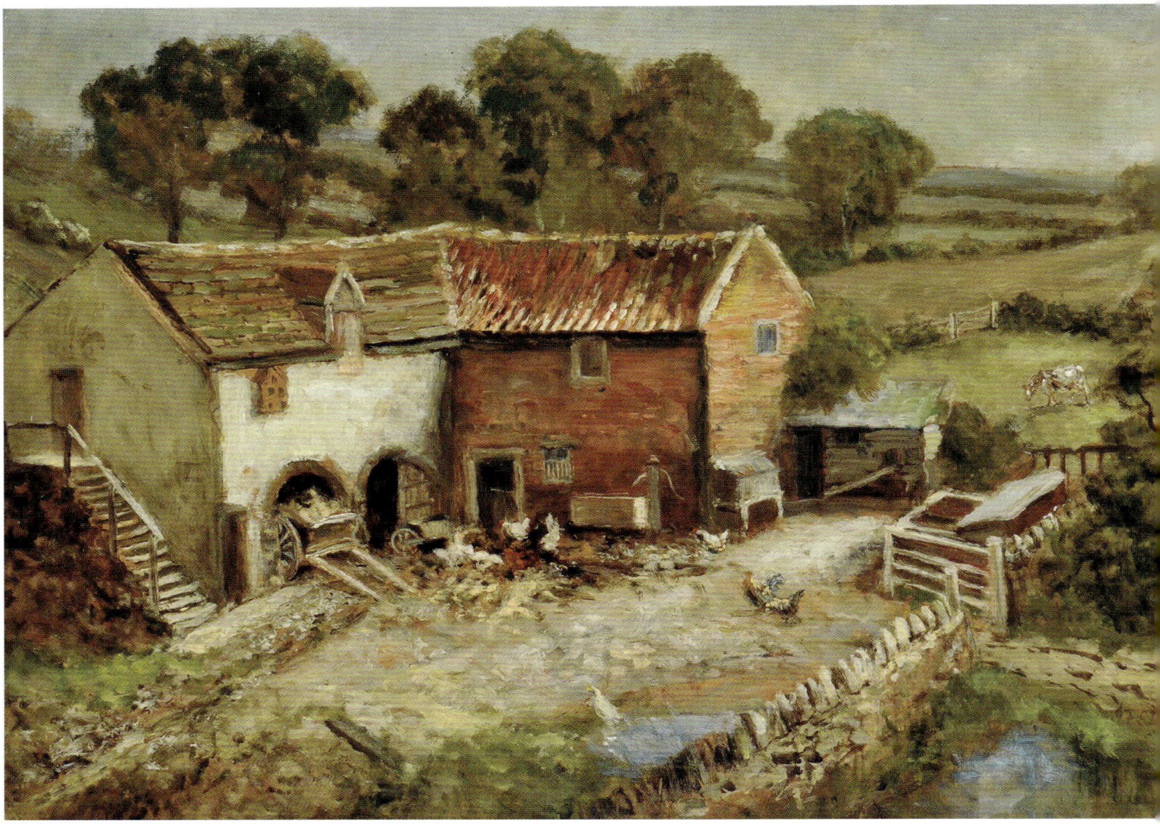

An example of one of Slater's oils based on his model farmyard. (Anderson & Garland)

career as an artist, was over. But a lengthy article about him in the *Shields Daily News* on March 23rd 1937 appeared to suggest the very opposite. Headlined 'Cullercoats Artist 80 on Friday', and accompanied by a photograph of him with one of his recent paintings of Cullercoats, it said: "Slowly recovering from an illness and allowed only two visitors a day, Mr John F. Slater, the famous Cullercoats artist, will be 80 years old on Good Friday and is longing to get hold of his brush and palette once again.

"His studio in his home at St Oswin's Avenue, Cullercoats, is just as he left it before he took ill five weeks ago. His paintings are piled around the walls leaving only a small square in the middle for the artist to stand at his easel, and the room is full of the artist's personality.

"I was unable to see Mr Slater when I called as his two visitors for that day had been fixed, but his son, Mr J. M. Slater, showed me around his father's room and described his work.

"A peep behind the scenes of an artist's studio holds a great fascination for the layman, the work preceding the finished picture arousing a mingling of interest and curiosity.

"Versatility is the most outstanding point of Slater's work for he believes that to justify his name an artist should be able to paint 'anything and everything'. Even at a casual glance at the paintings in his studio revealed that he had put this belief into practice. There were pictures of Cullercoats Village in all its aspects, paintings of moorland and rural scenes and innumerable paintings of vases of flowers. He has conveyed the beauty of vases of flowers by a splash of colour on a black background.

"The studio was cluttered up with palettes, brushes, paint bottles and two or three pipes just waiting for the master's hand to bring them to life again. 'Father just cannot bear being idle,' his son told me. 'He will only be happy when he can get downstairs into his studio and gets on painting again.

"'He is always dashing something or other off and refuses to be idle for one moment. His latest hobby is modelling and this is one of his latest efforts.'

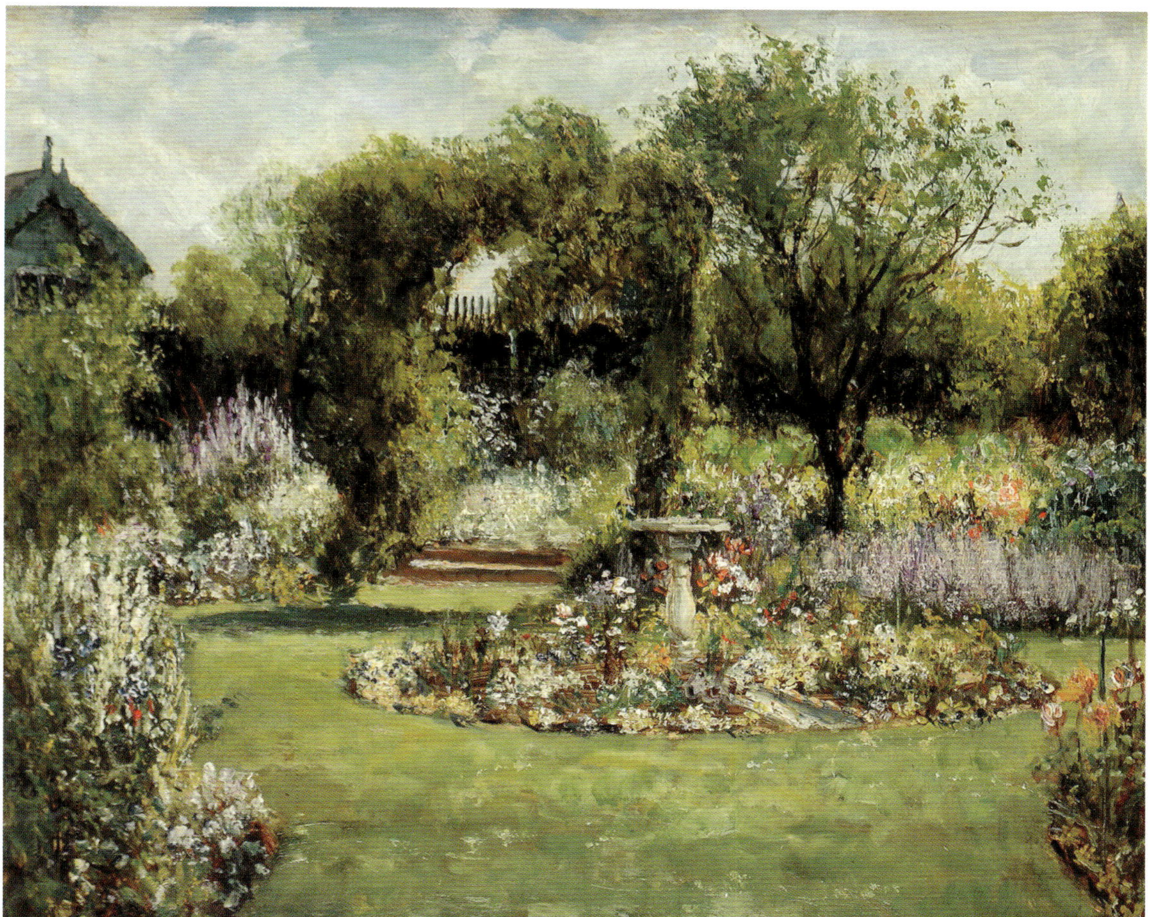

One of the local garden scenes which Slater began to paint when he could no longer travel far to paint his beloved seascapes. (Anderson & Garland)

"Mr Slater jnr then showed me an amazingly clever model of a farm, complete with barns and a yard. The model was on a fairly large scale and must have taken an enormous amount of patience.

"Every detail of a sleepy farmyard was shown, even to the untidiness of the rough hewn wall surrounding it with grass verges on the outside. He believes in detail, however, and spends several hours sketching his subject as a preliminary stage to the completion of an oil painting[26].

"Cullercoats and its inhabitants have been placed permanently on record by his vivid oil-paintings of the village in calm and storm and of the fishermen in their boats..."

Aware that their president's 80th birthday might well be his last, and to show their appreciation for all the work he had done on their behalf, North East Coast Art Club members decided to mark the occasion by presenting Slater with a cheque for £100, a silver rose bowl, an illuminated address and a decorated palette. Within days of their presentation he was dead, his life claimed by what was described on his death certificate as 'Coronary Artery Thrombosis and Chronic Myocarditis'. He died at 19 St Oswin's Avenue surrounded by his family on 23rd May 1937, almost 80 years and 2 months to the day since he'd first drawn breath on Newcastle's Rye Hill[27].

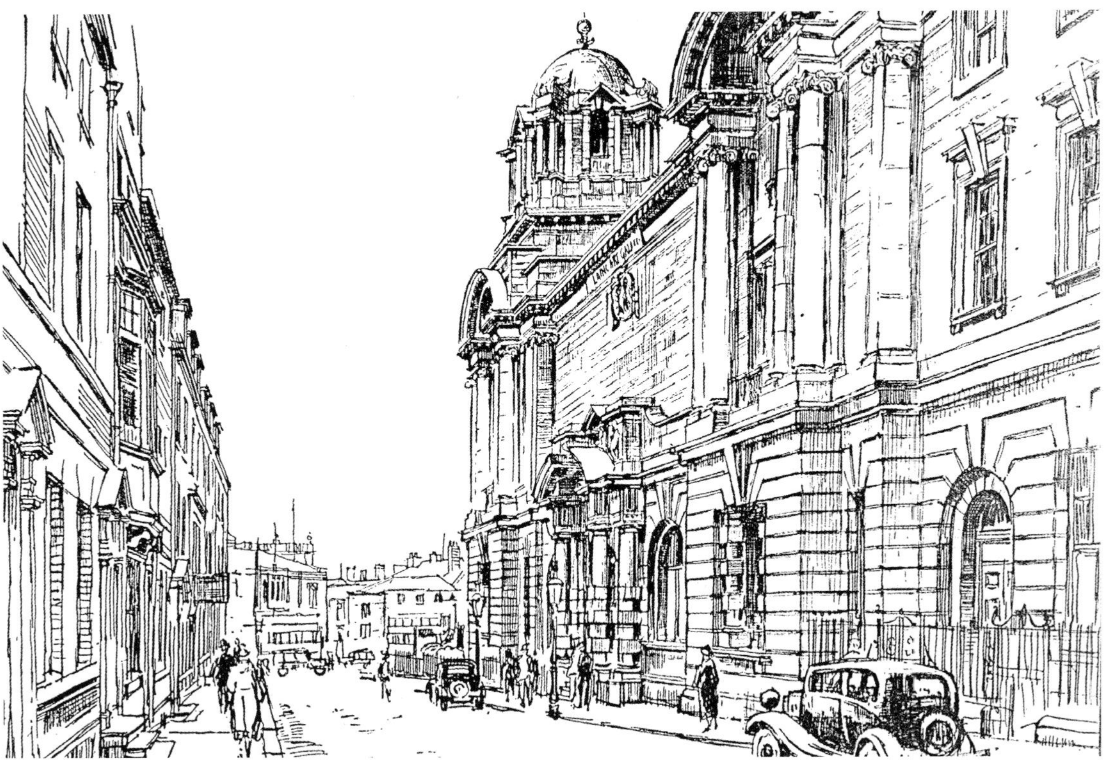

The Laing Art Gallery (right) as drawn by fellow North East artist Byron Dawson (1896-1968) for the North Mail, in 1936. Slater would show more than 100 works at the Laing between 1905 and his death in 1937. Opposite was the Pen & Palette Club to which he was a regular visitor.

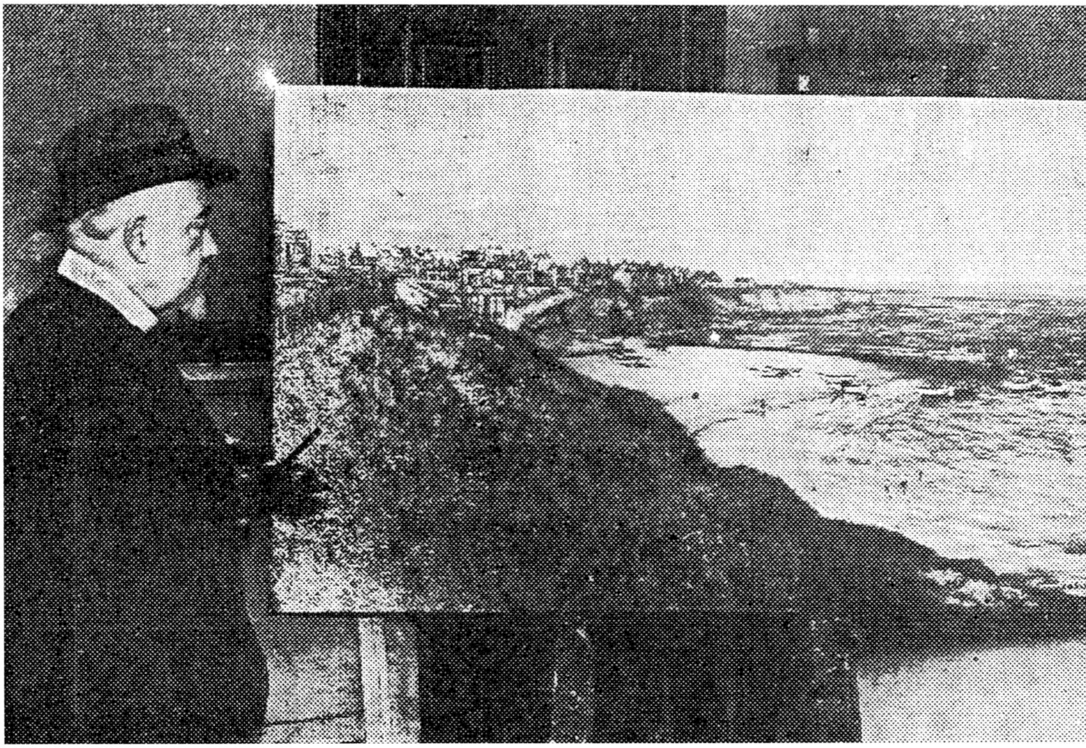

Slater with one of his last pictures of Cullercoats, as illustrated in the Shields Daily News, March 23rd 1937, a few weeks before his death.

Aftermath

Chapter Ten

They buried John Falconar Slater within sight, sound and smell of the subject he most loved to paint. His grave is in Whitley New Cemetery only a few hundred yards from the sea, and coincidentally the location of the wreck of the *California* he had painted in 1913 – the year the cemetery was opened.

He had purchased the grave plot some time previously, allowing space for his wife nearby, and as she left the graveside with her sons and daughters, she little knew how few would be the years before she joined him. The interment of her husband of 39 years had been preceded by a memorial service at the Fishermen's Mission at Cullercoats, and most of those present had joined the graveside with the family to bid farewell to possibly the best-known surviving member of the Cullercoats Colony; the previous claimant to this distinction – Robert Jobling – had already been interred nearby in 1923, and his artist wife Isabella (Thompson) three years later.

Following Slater's death his wife Sarah Ann, sons Thomas Waldron and John Martindale and daughters Mary Bertha and Agnes Dorothy continued to live at 19 St Oswin's Avenue. His daughters did not marry, and remained in the teaching profession until their respective resignations, Agnes Dorothy on 31st August 1961, from Murton Junior Mixed and Infants, after 40 years service with Tynemouth County Borough, and Mary Bertha, on 30th April 1963, from Ralph Gardner Secondary, after 42 years service with the County Borough.

Both sons are believed to have married. Thomas Waldron surviving until about 1970; John Martindale until 1979. They left St Oswin's Avenue after their marriages, the former around 1937, the latter around 1939. Their mother and sisters continued to live at the family home, the sisters alone after their mother's death in 1943 and burial alongside their father in Whitley New Cemetery.

When their brother Thomas Waldron died, the sisters decided to sell the house and move to the Tynedale village of Ryton to live with brother John Martindale, whose wife was in ill health and who eventually died. He followed her in 1979. The sisters sold his home (Burnaby Lodge) a short time after his death and bought a semi-detached house in nearby Burnaby Drive. Mary Bertha only survived a few months, and after living on her own for a few years, and falling into ill health Dorothy decided to sell the property and move into a nursing home (Wentworth Grange, Riding Mill, Northumberland) in 1986. Here she died in 1992 at the age of 91.

Slater left dozens of his paintings at St Oswin's Avenue on his death, along with his easels, palettes, brushes and other items. Most of these paintings etc remained in the family's possession until 1970 when John Martindale, who had inherited the bulk of the collection, entered ten of his father's paintings at Newcastle Fine Art Auctioneers Anderson & Garland on behalf of his sisters.

In anticipation of selling these works, and later other examples, John Martindale had written to the Royal Academy for a list of his father's Academy exhibits to incorporate in a slender leaflet giving brief details of his life and work. These details did not add substantially to those already in the public domain except those relating to his father's appearance and character: "He was short, broad, immensely strong, his hands were square and powerful. Not for him the velvet jacket and flowing tie. He habitually wore Harris tweeds… he was a great Christian, his love of humanity made all men - from the highest to the lowest - his friend."

John Martindale's remaining collection comprising mainly still lifes and flower studies, plus his father's easels etc, and the family's large collection of press cuttings covering their father's career, were sold by the same auctioneers in October 1980 following his death. Meanwhile, apparently unknown to his family, the National Maritime Museum, Greenwich, had acquired his large oil of the *North Sea from Whitley Bay*. It had formerly been owned by London's Chevron Club and was gifted to the Museum on its closure in 1975. When offered to its then curator Teddy Archibald he remarked to the Club: "The Slater I liked very much and would be happy to accept it."

The years since 1980 have seen a steadily increasing appreciation of Slater's work (and a commensurate rise in their price at auction), partly due to a long overdue recognition of the Impressionist qualities of many of his paintings. Sadly, however, this recognition has not so

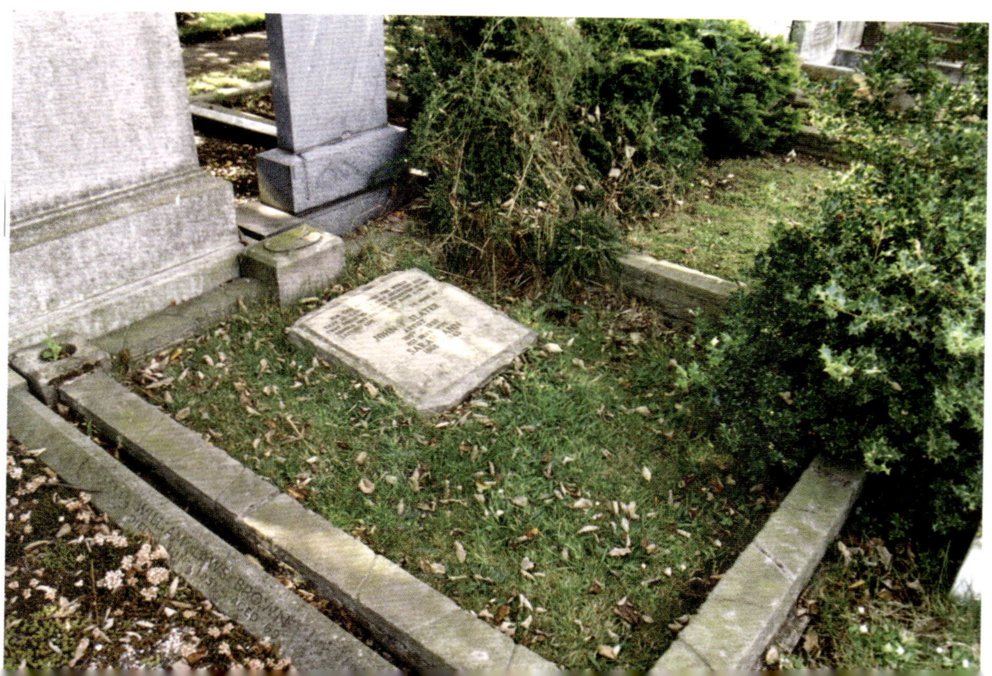

Slater's and his wife's graves in Whitley New Cemetery.

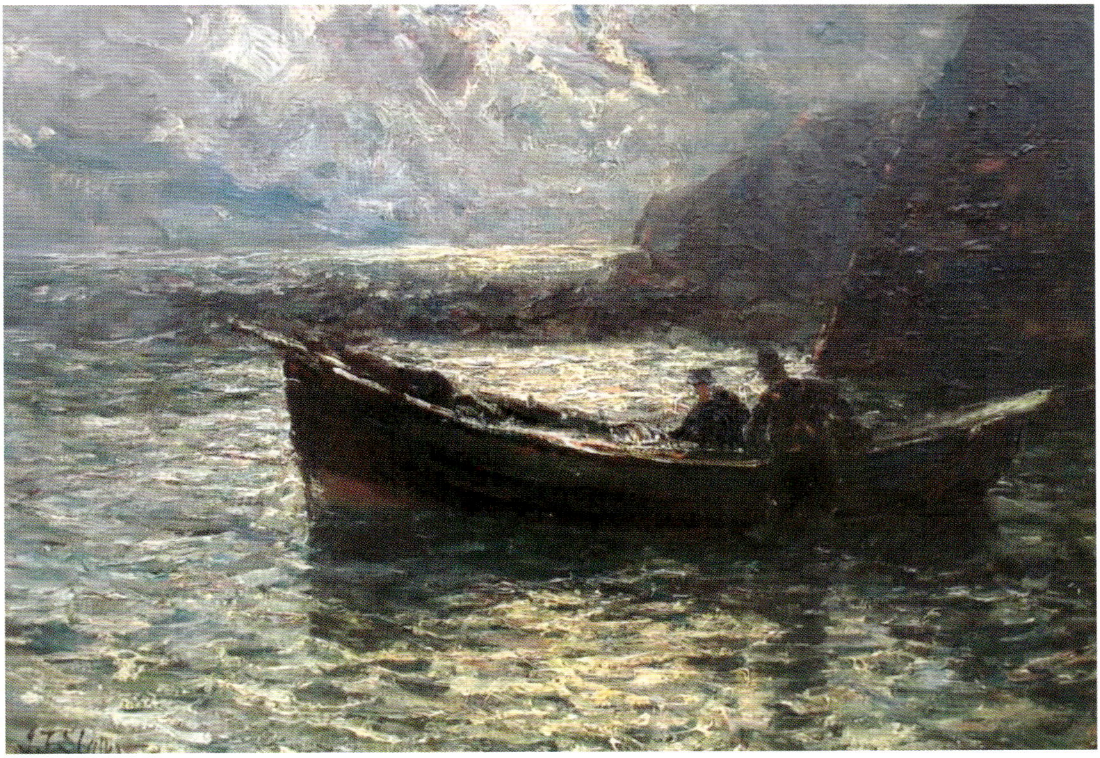

A typical late example of Slater's Impressionist work. (T B & R Jordan)

far led to a major exhibition of his work, although a small, selective showing of some of its finest examples, staged in collaboration with the author by George Lilly, director of the Vicarage Cottage Gallery in North Shields, in 1987, to mark the 50th anniversary of the artist's death, went some way to making up for this omission, as did the inclusion of some of his finest works in the Laing's 2003 exhibition: *Cullercoats – A North East Colony of Artists*, and their illustration in the accompanying publication of that name by Laura Newton, with Abigail Booth Gerdts. However, Slater's true place within the framework of the Colony has still not been fully established.

He never really perceived himself as a member of any group apart from that associated with the North East Coast Art Club – he was far too independent a man to accept this sort of branding. But the authors of the book make a good case for the justification of his inclusion, referring to him on ten occasions within it, starting with his description as one of the 'main professional artists of the group' comprising also: "Henry Hetherington Emmerson, Robert Jobling, Arthur Hardwick Marsh, Isa Thompson, George Horton, and John Charlton."

These references to him in the book are both perceptive and illuminating of this claim, but it is all too easy in similarly treating the other artists in the extended Group, for his important role in the Colony to be lost in importance. A reading of the book's text, and particularly its section on the "Main Artists of Cullercoats", for instance, reveals on examination that Slater lived in the area around the village itself for more years continuously than any other member. His problem in being regarded as a quintessential member has, perhaps, lain in his choice of subject, Slater largely foregoing the popular studies of fisherfolk and their activities, favoured by Robert Jobling, Henry Hetherington Emmerson, and Ralph Hedley, and concentrated instead on studies of the sea from local vantage points, or broad topographical pieces. Indeed, not until these artists had passed away, along with their subjects, did he begin to include figures, and then of the general public.

His reluctance to paint the same subjects as Robert Jobling, for instance (who incidentally was as much fascinated by the similar scenes to Cullercoats he and his wife Isa found at Staithes, down the coast) is all the more surprising given that Slater possibly had a unique relationship with these very subjects. In his *Odds and Ends*, in his chapter headed "Amusing Experiences", he says: "I have had happy times amongst the fisher folk and have had their hearty interest because my work in the stress of weather which those hardy Northerners know so well in the pursuit of their livelihood, with all its disappointments and dangers."

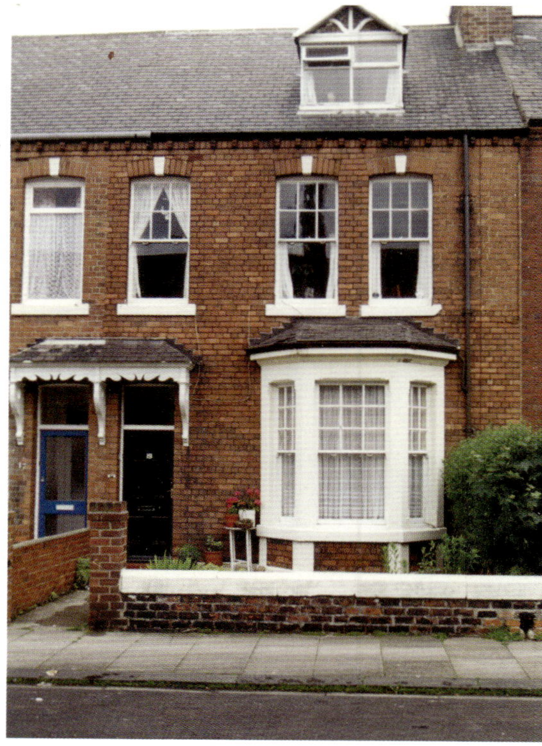

In addition to all the foregoing arguments for him to be given his true status, he was the last important player in the Newton/Gerdts study to die (George Horton did not die until thirteen years later but had, in any event lived away from the North East for many years). Slater had, after all, been the only member of the Group, who, in his sweeping 1905 panorama of the village, pictured the backdrop to its collective activities. This, not to mention, his much closer-up view of this scene in his mixed media work *Cullercoats*, painted in 1910, and illustrated full page in colour in the Newton/Gerdts study of the Colony, and on page 51 of this book.

Slater's contribution to maintaining the legacy of the Colony until his death is something also worthy of research, both as an individual long-term member of the group and the creator of The North East Coast Art Club in 1920. Admittedly, and by its title, it proclaimed itself as a club not solely concerned with Cullercoats as a subject, but the village continued to be substantially represented in its exhibited work for most of the years of its subsequent existence.

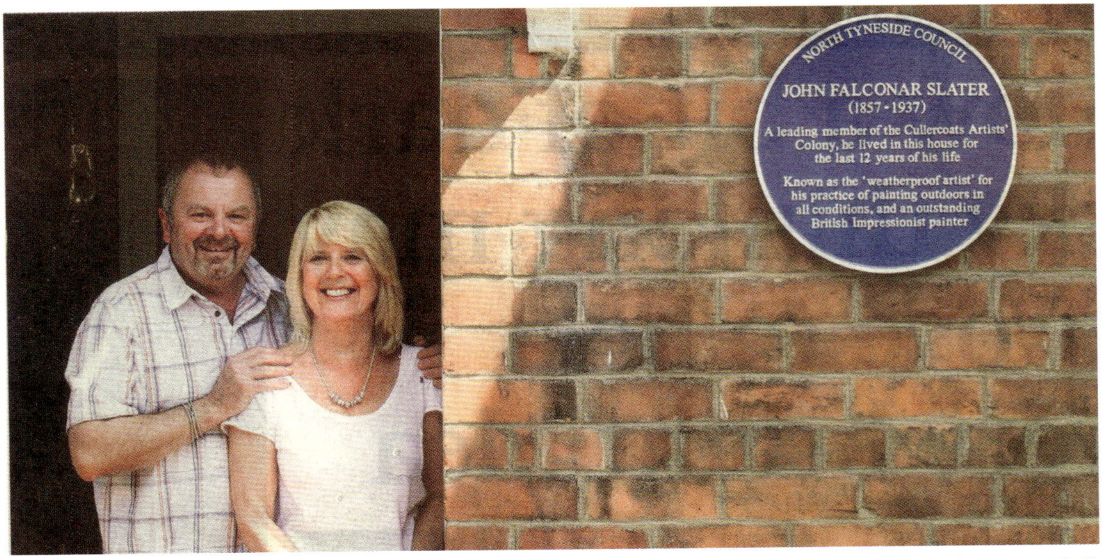

Above: Steve and Alwyne Barrigan after the unveiling of the commemorative plaque on their home at 19 St Oswin's Avenue in 2012. (Newcastle Journal). Opposite page: The house before the addition of the plaque.

Slater was one of the most prolific artists the North East has ever produced[28] and his impressively large number of works and their varied range of subject matter makes it difficult to pigeonhole him as an artist. Credit must therefore be given to North Tyneside Council for the wording of the plaque it placed on his one-time Cullercoats home in 2012 at the invitation of its owners Steve and Alwyne Barrigan, summarising as it does so succinctly, his main claims to distinction as an artist:

John Falconar Slater

(1857-1937)

A leading member of the

Cullercoats Artists' Colony, he lived in this house

for the last 12 years of his life.

Known as the 'weatherproof artist'

for his practice of painting outdoors

in all conditions,

and an outstanding British Impressionist painter

Notes

1. In registering his birth his parents chose as his Christian names 'John' after his paternal grandfather, and 'Falconar', his grandmother's maiden name. His mother's parents were Thomas Horn, Newcastle music seller (and later grain merchant), and Margaret Falconar. Curiously, in announcing Slater's birth in the *Newcastle Courant*, 27th March 1857, it read: "In Elswick West Villas, on 25th inst., the wife of Mr Thos. Slater, of a son" i.e. a day earlier than his recorded date of birth.

2. Slater's sister Mary, born in 1853, had by now died aged five.

3. Some measure of the teaching success of the Academy may be gained from the fact that even after Wilson's death in 1919, and while still Principal, it continued to the mid-1950s, when the building was taken over by the Northumberland and Durham Adoption Society. Demolished in the early 1960s, it was partly swallowed up in the University of Northumbria's development.

4. A further dozen in Gateshead were also in operation, one of which, in Swalwell, is listed as being a subsidiary of the Forth Street Mill.

5. Interestingly, another branch of the Slater family was heavily involved in the trade. Directories of the period identify relative William Slater as both Proprietor and Mourning Coach Proprietor. The firm later became well known as operators of a taxi service which continued to be based principally at Newcastle Central Station until late in the last century.

6. Flintoff was one of the witnesses at the marriage of Slater's parents, Thomas Slater (b.1820), and Mary Busher Horn (b.1823), on 15th August 1850. For an account of his life and work see p.126 *The Artists of Northumbria*, Third Edition, 2005, by the author.

7. They would exhibit together at the Bewick Club in 1893, she showing an oil: *Touching Up*.

8. Slater also painted another Boer War related work: *Challenging the Heights*, at around the same time. Several other prominent North East artists also painted pictures related to the conflict, notably John Charlton (1849-1917), with his 1900 Royal Academy exhibit: *Routed: Boers Retreating*, and Ralph Hedley (1848-1913), in the same year at the Academy, *The Reservist's Wife*.

9. Launched by *Chronicle* editor William Edwin Adams (1832-1906) and dedicated to the protection of birds and all living things, he chose as his imaginary figurehead and alias for his weekly column on the Society's activities, a delightful gentleman named Uncle Toby, in

Lawrence Sterne's book *Tristram Shandy*. Despite widespread enquiries Slater's portrayal of Uncle Toby with members of the Society has not yet been located.

10. The circumstances by which he came to choose the same building as that already used as a studio location by fellow-artist Elizabeth Cameron Mawson (1849-1939), the daughter of successful Gateshead businessman and later Sheriff of Newcastle, John Mawson, who owned 13 Mosley Street, are not known. Certainly the two artists must have been acquainted before this happened, possibly through attending local exhibitions at which they were each showing work.

11. The couple's choice of Grindleford was probably determined more by Slater than his new bride. He took his painting materials with him and produced several oils, one of which in the family's ownership for many years portrayed their honeymoon accommodation in the village. A second visit to the area in the 1880s involving a stay at Ashton under Lyne, encouraged Slater to show examples of his work at Manchester City Art Gallery and the Walker Art Gallery, Liverpool.

12. His sister, Bertha, had died in 1882, aged 19, and his brother Waldron Story, having married in 1904, had sailed for New Zealand with his wife Mary (Crosby). He died there in 1916 leaving a large family to be brought up by Mary.

13. *Shields Daily News,* 24th August 1906.

14. *Shields Daily News,* 27th February 1911.

15. *Artists of the Northern Counties* exhibition catalogue, Laing Art Gallery, 1913.

16. *Artists of the Northern Counties* exhibition catalogue, Laing Art Gallery, 1913.

17. The resulting oil was exhibited at the *Artists of the Northern Counties* exhibition, Laing Art Gallery, in the same year in which it was painted (No.50: *Remnants of the California*).

18. This in addition to staging several exhibitions of his work at 15 The Esplanade. See *Shields Daily News*, 27th December 1917, for note of typical example.

19. It is possible that Slater painted Creed's portrait in the studio he rented at 2 St Nicholas Building in Newcastle from 1921-23, while living at 42 Lish Avenue, Whitley Bay, and to coincide with the 10th anniversary of his sitter's invention having been introduced to Fleet Street, London. The location of the portrait has not yet been established despite widespread enquiries, including with Croydon Archives, which holds a large collection of Creed material, including letters, photographs of the inventor, etc.

20. The honour from the King referred to was in respect of this bravery, and was conferred

on 30th June 1924, when he, along with fellow crew members, was received at Buckingham Palace as part of the RNLI centenary celebrations, and received the newly instituted Empire Gallantry Medal. The wish expressed in this editorial that the portrait be displayed at the seaside has for several years been fulfilled by its display at the RNLI's Tynemouth Lifeboat Station at North Shields. Smith died three years after his portrait was painted, aged 78.

21. Kenneth Glover (1887-1966) was also an artist, and portrait subject of Slater. His oil of Glover was shown at *The Artists of the Northern Counties* exhibition at the Laing Art Gallery in 1923.

22. This was not the first time that particulars of Slater's career as an artist had appeared in a prestigious publication. These were included, together with a photographic portrait in *Northumberland & Durham at the Opening of the Twentieth Century*, published in 1905. Consisting of what its editor James Jamieson described as 'Contemporary Biographies', it included leading members of 'the Nobility & Gentry, Art, Literature, Science, Scholastic, etc. Among fellow artists included were Ralph Hedley (1848-1913), and Arthur Hardwick Marsh (1842-1909).

23. This was probably the largest exhibition of works by famous artists of the past and present staged in the North East of England to date. However, in the *North Mail*, in a special supplement on the exhibition generally, published May14th 1929, it was quoted that 'several special aims of the committee responsible for the exhibition have been achieved. The first is the due recognition of the North East Coast artists past and present.' Around one fifth of the some 677 plus totally on show were, in the event, by local artists of the past and present, 14 out of the 72 illustrations in the accompanying catalogue being devoted to such works.

24. It is difficult to believe that he actually painted this on the spot, given its enormous size, and the task involved in transporting the canvas. Hexham Station is several hundred yards away from the spot identified, and presuming it to have been carried on the train from Newcastle and returned in the same way, a large cart would have been necessary in both directions. He painted several similar views of the town in his career, an earlier and smaller version being presented to South Shields Art Gallery and Museum by Thomas Reed before the Laing received theirs.

25. Slater's portrait of 'Scraper Smith', and his widely known association with Watson led many to misguidedly believe that the artist provided the illustration for the label on the company's tinned fish products. Watson, however, contradicts this by his own account of its origins in his autobiography *My Life*, published in 1937.

26. Slater's practice in using this, and earlier of his model farms, as a basis of his compositions is evident in a number of his later works, when he clearly was not as readily able to sketch real-life versions on the spot. This particular model he sent for exhibition to *The Artists of the Northern Counties* exhibition at the Laing Art Gallery, in 1936.

27. Just before his death Slater planned to send two of his latest works to the 1937 *Artists of the Northern Counties* exhibition, at the Laing. His family implemented this intention, the two works in question being an oil: *Morning Light*, and a watercolour: *River Tyne.* They appeared in the catalogue as being by the late J. F. Slater. By coincidence, or otherwise, a bust of him by Whitley Bay sculptor Mayjor Gaunt Lofthouse was also shown on this occasion.

28. The author and the artist's daughter Dorothy once calculated that he could have produced as many as 10,000 works i.e. oils, watercolours, gouaches, etc in his almost half century career as an artist, these ranging from his highly finished Royal Academy and other venue exhibits, to those she admitted "he dashed off" just to help keep the family supported before she, her sister and brothers, were able to contribute to its income through their respective employments.

Paintings accepted for Royal Academy Summer Exhibitions

Year	No.	Title
1889	966	The Boat Landing.
1891	822	Ploughing.
1892	818	Going to Market.
1899	186	A Fresh Breeze.
1900	420	Fleeting Sunshine in the Vale.
1903	699	"And all the air a solemn stillness holds."
1904	16	The Calm that Evening Knew.
1905	262	"The strong winds of day do mingle sea and clouds."
1906	86	"You hear the breakers' sullen roar, and watch the waves ascend in spray."
1908	173	The Northumbrian Coast.
	907	Running for Refuge.
1911	327	After the Storm: Northumberland Coast.
1912	357	A Rift in the Clouds.
	723	The North Sea, Whitley Bay.
1914	525	A Fresh Day on the North-East Coast.
	1307	Morning After the Storm.
1915	1013	An Expression of Morning.
	1034	An Expression of Night.
	1253	An Expression of the Glen.
1917	616	The Snowstorm.
1924	637	The North Sea.
1936	338	The River Tyne.

Other exhibitions for which work accepted

Gateshead Fine Art & Industrial Exhibition, 1883; Bewick Club, 1884-1918; Royal Mining, Engineering and Industrial Exhibition, Newcastle, 1887; Central Exchange Art Gallery, Newcastle, 1892; Carlisle Art Gallery, 1896; Tynemouth Fine Art Association, and South Shields Art Club, 1885-1896; Walker Art Gallery, Liverpool, and Manchester City Art Gallery, 1885-1887; Exhibition of Local Artists (Artists War Fund), Newcastle 1900; Artists of the Northern Counties Exhibition, Newcastle, 1905-1937; Royal Scottish Academy, 1920; North East Coast Exhibition, Newcastle, 1929; Montrose Art Exhibition, Angus, Scotland, 1929; North East Coast Art Club, Whitley Bay, 1920-1936; Four-man Exhibition (Thomas Bowman Garvie, Frank Thomas Carter, George Horton, and John Falconar Slater), Newcastle, 1934.

Oil Paintings in Public Ownership

Bank of England Museum

Stormy Sea.

Darlington Borough Art Collection

Landscape.

Durham University

Landscape with trees and stream.

Government Art Collection

Trawlers, South Shields on the Tyne, 1913.

Laing Art Gallery, Newcastle upon Tyne

Quayside at North Shields, c.1890-1910.

The Wood Cart, c.1890-1910.

Seascape, c.1890-1910.

Laing Art Gallery, Newcastle upon Tyne - Continued

Winter Scene, c.1890-1910.

Two Horses and a Caravan, c.1900-1920.

Seascape, 1905.

Cullercoats, Northumberland, 1910.

A Glen.

Cottage and Stream.

Hexham, Northumberland.

Landscape with Mountain Stream.

Landscape with Windmill.

North Shields, North Tyneside.

St Mary's Lighthouse.

Seascape.

Seascape.

Seascape.

Seascape.

Tynemouth Pier.

Lancaster City Museums, Lancaster

Winter Weather.

National Maritime Museum, London

View of Whitley Bay, Northumberland.

North Lanarkshire Council Museums and Heritage Service

Cobles in the Haven, Cullercoats.

North Tyneside Council

Stormy Sea at Cullercoats.

Shipley Art Gallery, Gateshead

Landscape with Torrent.

Lombardy Poplars.

River Scene with Pink Mountain.

Scottish Highlands.

South Shields Museum and Art Gallery

Afterglow, Hexham, Northumberland.

Cullercoats Bay.

Sunderland Museum and Winter Gardens

Seascape, c.1890-1920.

Woodland Scene.